THE TERRY LECTURES

*Israelis and the Jewish Tradition*

# Israelis
## and the
# Jewish Tradition

*An Ancient People Debating
Its Future*

DAVID HARTMAN

*Yale University Press*    *New Haven & London*

Published with assistance from the foundation established in memory of Philip Hamilton McMillan of the Class of 1894, Yale College.

Designed by James J. Johnson and set in Stemple Garamond types by Tseng Information Systems, Inc., Durham, North Carolina.

Printed in the United States of America by Sheridan Books, Chelsea, Michigan.

*Library of Congress Cataloging-in-Publication Data*

Hartman, David, 1931–

Israelis and the Jewish tradition : an ancient people debating its future / David Hartman.

p. cm. — (The Terry lectures)

Includes bibliographical references and index.

ISBN 0-300-08378-5 (alk. paper)

1. Jews—Israel—Identity. 2. Judaism—Israel. 3. Secularism— Israel. 4. Zionism—Philosophy. 5. Maimonides, Moses, 1135-1204. 6. Judah, ha-Levi, 12th cent. I. Title. II. Series.

DS143 .H27 2000

305.89'2405694—dc21                    00-036825

A catalogue record for this book is available from the British Library.

The paper in this book meets the guidelines for permanence and durability of the Committee on Production Guidelines for Book Longevity of the Council on Library Resources.

10  9  8  7  6  5  4  3  2  1

# The Dwight Harrington Terry Foundation Lectures on Religion in the Light of Science and Philosophy

The deed of gift declares that "the object of this foundation is not the promotion of scientific investigation and discovery, but rather the assimilation and interpretation of that which has been or shall be hereafter discovered, and its application to human welfare, especially by the building of the truths of science and philosophy into the structure of a broadened and purified religion. The founder believes that such a religion will greatly stimulate intelligent effort for the improvement of human conditions and the advancement of the race in strength and excellence of character. To this end it is desired that a series of lectures be given by men eminent in their respective departments, on ethics, the history of civilization and religion, biblical research, all sciences and branches of knowledge which have an important bearing on the subject, all the great laws of nature, especially of evolution . . . also such interpretations of literature and sociology as are in accord with the spirit of this foundation, to the end that the Christian spirit may be nurtured in the fullest light of the world's knowledge and that mankind may be helped to attain its highest possible welfare and happiness upon this earth." The present work constitutes the latest volume published on this foundation.

*To Bobbie*

# Contents

Preface     vii

CHAPTER ONE   Crisis and Tradition     1

CHAPTER TWO   The God of History in
     Yehuda Halevi     26

CHAPTER THREE   The Cosmic God in
     Maimonides     52

CHAPTER FOUR   Rabbinic Foundations of
     Maimonides' Thought     88

CHAPTER FIVE   Halakhic Sobriety and
     Inclusiveness     123

References     167

Index     171

# Preface

I was honored to receive the invitation from Dean Richard Wood of the Yale University Divinity School to deliver the Terry Lectures of 1998. Both the title—"A Nation in Search of Its Soul"—and the date of the lectures indicated that Yale University wished to honor the state of Israel on the fiftieth anniversary of its founding. I decided to approach the lectures' bold theme by clarifying the crisis facing secular and religious Zionists in Israel today.

After the Six-Day War, the attitudes of many religious Zionists in Israel underwent a dramatic change. Their religious passion became focused exclusively on building settlements throughout the Land of Israel (Judea and Samaria). In that way, they believed, they would help realize the biblical, messianic promise. They viewed Israel's victory in the Six-Day War as a divine affirmation of their participation in the secular Zionist revolution, which in many ways had undermined traditional Judaism.

In reclaiming the land, Zionists were, in effect, reclaiming the biblical covenant. In settling Judea and Samaria they were expressing loyalty to God's covenantal election of Israel and to the eternal bond between God, the land, and the destiny of the Jewish people. The passion felt by many religious Zionists was also fueled by their belief that their actions were vindicating two thousand years of Jewish prayers for redemption and return to the Land of Israel.

The commencement of the current peace process and the growing awareness of the Palestinian sovereignty over parts of the Land of Israel shattered a central ideological tenet of this form of religious Zionism. It became evident that territorial compromise was the only realistic way of reaching a practical peaceful solution to the tragic conflict between Israelis and Palestinians. Consequently, many in Israel's religious Zionist community find themselves searching for a new theology of history, one that can give meaning to their Zionist commitments from a perspective outside the territorial, messianic framework.

Nonobservant Israelis, who have long felt estranged from their Jewish heritage, are also experiencing an existential crisis. Normalization and nationalism no longer have the significance they once did in providing meaning and purpose for Jewish identities. Consequently, many secular Zionists wish to engage their tradition—but not in the traditional Orthodox manner.

These Israelis are immersed in the modern world. They seek to embrace the best of modern Western values; they therefore consider neither the insulated cultural mindset of the "haredi" (ultra-Orthodox communities) in Jerusalem and Bnei Brak nor a secular Western way of life to be viable. But the choice between ghettoization or assimilation into secular Western culture is not the only option. Along with many Israelis, I believe that we can find new ways of integrating the Jewish tradition with modern culture and values.

My involvement as an educator in both these communities has led me to a view of religious Zionism grounded in a normative covenantal framework that is independent of messianism. Events in history need not be appreciated only as signposts that point to a new eschatological future and mark the progress of God's redemptive purpose. Historical events can become religiously significant to the degree that they bear witness to the foundational moments of the Jewish tradition. The religious significance of an event can be revealed in the challenge it offers us to interpret and draw new meaning from the powerful narrative and normative frameworks of the tradition.

In this book I have organized my Terry Lectures around the idea of Judaism as a way of life rather than as a system of faith driven by the idea of messianic redemption or cultural ghettoization. The first and last chapters, "Crisis and Tradition" and "Halakhic Sobriety and Inclusiveness," analyze the history of the problem that both religious and secular Zionists face and offer suggestions to help mitigate this problem and guide those who experience the crisis as a personal, spiritual dilemma.

In the chapters on the twelfth-century philosophers Yehuda Halevi and Moses Maimonides I discuss two of the most important approaches to Judaism and the Jewish tradition, which have shaped Jewish religious consciousness from the Middle Ages onward. In addition to his well-known religious poetry, Halevi's book *The Kuzari: The Book of Refutation and Proof on Behalf of the Despised Religion* continues to be read and studied by Jews to this day, while Maimonides is perhaps the most widely known Jewish philosopher and halakhist in the world. His systematic classification and codification of Jewish law, the *Mishneh Torah,* and his monumental philosophical work *The Guide of the Perplexed* are unparalleled milestones in the intellectual and legal-halakhic history of the Jewish people. In my chapters on Halevi and Maimonides, I try to familiarize the reader with their respective philosophical and spiritual orientations, which represent two major, very different religious sensibilities in the Judaic tradition.

Halevi's event-based theology had its roots in the biblical tradition, whereas Maimonides' philosophical religious worldview may be understood as reflecting certain important features of the talmudic tradition. Halevi's religious sensibility is energized by a quest for distinctiveness and uniqueness, a desire to sustain and confirm the fundamental meaning of Jewish destiny through a revelation of Judaism's uniqueness. Maimonides, on the other hand, encourages the cultivation of a religious sensibility that does not thrive on distinctiveness and uniqueness but is able—and actively tries—to translate the Jewish religion and way of life into universal categories of rationality and human psychology. The particularity of Judaism has significance for Maimonides without dubious claims about the distinctive logic of revelation and divine authority.

The Maimonidean sensibility can be regarded as a meaningful precedent and model for individuals seeking ways to reclaim their tradition while at the same time sharing in the values and cultural traditions of the broader human community. Maimonides' religious sensibility may also provide us with a basis for appreciating and celebrating the rebirth of the state of Israel without making exaggerated messianic claims for the event.

Of the two, Halevi is closer to the spirit of the biblical tradition in which God's directives to His people are revealed through events in history, and redemption becomes a key energizing and organizing framework for Judaic self-understanding. From Maimonides' perspective, messianism is not the predominant organizing principle that makes Judaism intelligible and significant. In fact, in *The Guide of the Perplexed,* Maimonides shows little or no interest in messianism or historic redemption. Instead, he is deeply drawn and committed to a philosophic spirituality influenced by Aristotle and the Islamic Aristotelians in which the study of nature and philosophy —the disciplines known then as physics and metaphysics—constituted the path to the highest form of religious worship.

In the chapter "Rabbinic Foundations of Maimonides' Thought," I argue that the talmudic tradition provided an appropriate framework for Maimonides to incorporate the God of Aristotle into the Jewish tradition. Had Judaism consisted solely of the Bible, Maimonides' intellectual and religious undertaking would have been—some scholars claim it actually was—unintelligible from a Jewish point of view. The distinction between Athens and Jerusalem would have been far too radical and thus unbridgeable in the quest for a plausible way of combining Aristotle's God of being with the prophetic God of history. The Talmud, however, provided a suitable context for Maimonides' philosophical religious outlook in that it shifted the focus of the Jewish tradition from a revelation-centered, event-based theology to a Torah/text-centered religious way of life. In this new environment learning and developing the Torah were the main organizing components of experiencing God's presence in history. The rabbinic tradition thus provided a framework for expressing a religious passion that was not nurtured or driven by the dramatic interventions of God in history.

In discussing Maimonides and Halevi, I do not claim that they would necessarily have agreed with my application of their thought to the modern situation. As in other cases of dealing with the Jewish philosophical tradition, I do not claim that my analyses and interpretations are what the author intended, only that what the author said or wrote makes the interpretation or application plausible.

One could say that the task of Jewish philosophy is not only to present an intellectual history of Jewish ideas and arguments but also to carry the discussion within the tradition further, to recognize and explore what it makes possible, undeterred by the fear that the discussion might go beyond what past participants intended. Talmudic and medieval writers and thinkers do not, ought not to, and cannot control all the implications and consequences of their creative contributions to the tradition. This is the approach I shall take in evaluating the place of Maimonides, Halevi, and the talmudic tradition in these lectures.

My analysis of the spiritual struggle in Israel today is based on my experience teaching and living in Israeli society. It is not a sociological study or a comparative analysis of prevalent beliefs and attitudes in Israeli society. So although some Israelis may neither recognize themselves in the models and types presented nor share the opinions and attitudes described, I am confident that many others will accept them as an accurate insight into their personal, existential struggles.

Israel today is a divided society composed of many social, cultural, and spiritual elements. There are secular Israelis who believe that their existing culture, the Hebrew language, the flourishing of Hebrew literature and other art forms, and the establishment of a nation are sufficient to provide meaning for their Israeli identities. I do not argue against this position because I profoundly respect the achievements of secular Israelis who rebelled against Jewish tradition. I reject the view that there can be no meaning or purpose to personal and cultural ways of life in Israel that ignore traditional Judaism.

Nevertheless, I am of the opinion that the secular option no longer works for many Israelis who wish to reconnect with their Jewish spiritual heritage. One of the tasks of a Jewish philosopher living in Israel is to articulate a vision of Judaism that can empower and energize these spiritual and intellectual needs. This is the spirit in which I wrote these lectures.

I am deeply grateful to my colleagues in Israel who read my revisions of the lectures and offered insightful suggestions for preparing them for publication. I am especially indebted to Hanina Ben-Menachem, Menachem Fisch, Moshe Halbertal, Warren Harvey, Moshe Idel, Menachem Lorberbaum, Ehud Luz, Shlomo Naeh, and Avi Sagi. I would also like to express my gratitude to my colleagues in the diaspora, Barry Kogan, Hilary Putnam, and Michael Walzer, whose comments were very helpful in bringing this work to its final form.

I deeply appreciate the thoughtful criticism and suggestions of all my colleagues. It is a privilege to work and write at the Shalom Hartman Institute in Jerusalem, where one finds a community of scholars prepared to engage the creative work of others in a critical yet sympathetic way that can only improve its quality.

I would also like to express my appreciation and gratitude to my student, research assistant, and philosophical colleague Elliott Yagod. His devotion and cooperation in preparing these lectures for publication were invaluable, both technically and intellectually.

Words cannot express my appreciation for my wife, Bobbie, who has always been a source of strength and an intellectual companion throughout the years of our marriage. It was Bobbie's deep commitment and determination that enabled our family to move successfully from Montreal to Israel and to make Israel our permanent home. Her steadfast love for Israel enabled me to overcome the manic-depressive experiences I underwent in attempting to build a new life there. It is to Bobbie that I dedicate this work.

*Israelis and the Jewish Tradition*

# CHAPTER ONE

# Crisis and Tradition

The dramatic events of the twentieth century have altered the traditional interpretation of exile for Jewish self-understanding. Before the advent of modern Zionism, the biblical story of the Exodus from Egypt had served as the dominant paradigm of Jewish history; it implied that change in the Jewish people's exilic condition would occur only through the radical intervention of God. On the night of the Passover seder we read the following blessing: "Blessed are You, Lord our God, Ruler of the universe, Who redeemed us and redeemed our ancestors from Egypt, and enabled us to reach this night, to eat thereon *Matzah* and bitter herbs. So may the Lord our God and God of our ancestors enable us to reach other holidays and festivals in peace, happy in the building of Your city Jerusalem, and joyful in Your service. There may we partake of the Passover offerings. We shall then sing unto You a new song of praise for our redemption and salvation. Blessed are You, O Lord, Who redeemed Israel" (Passover Haggadah). Liberation from exile was not to be realized through human efforts. When asked whether he celebrated Israel's Independence Day, a noted rabbi once answered: "I have only one Independence Day—the liberation day known as Passover."

The prevailing theological understanding of Jewish history linked the conditions of exile, homelessness, and political powerlessness with sin. "Because of our sins we were exiled from our country and banished far from our land. Our Father, our King, speedily reveal thy glorious majesty to us; shine forth and be exalted over us in the sight of all the living. Unite our scattered people from among the nations; gather our dispersed from the far ends of the earth. Bring us to Zion thy city with ringing song, to Jerusalem thy sanctuary with everlasting joy" (Siddur [daily prayer book]). The upshot of this was the belief that historical change could come about only by the spiritual transformation of the people or an act of divine grace. "All the prophets charged the people concerning repentance. Only through repentance will Israel be redeemed, and the Torah already offered the assurance that Israel will, in the closing period of his exile, finally repent, and thereupon be immediately redeemed" (Maimonides, "Laws of Repentance" 7:5).

Zionism, on the other hand, represented a transformation of this traditional form of self-understanding. Its fundamental message was: If you wish to change your exilic condition, you must learn how nations emerge and survive. If you wish to return to the land, don't wait for a miracle or a prophet to arise. Build agricultural schools, improve your economic base and your knowledge of banking and finance. Develop the art of self-defense, of modern warfare; become experts in military matters; in a word, master whatever it takes to build a viable state. Secular Zionism completely de-mythologized the Jewish people's sense of who they were. It contradicted accepted patterns of thought by asserting that exile was not necessarily grounded in sin or observance of the Torah commandments but could be the result of a failure to exploit the political, social, economic, and military conditions required for nation building.

What was interesting about this radical revolt against tradition was that it was intended to be realized in the selfsame land of the biblical promise that the traditionalists sought. My favorite image for capturing this paradox is that of the teenager who announces to his parents: "I'm tired of living with you. I'm sick of all the stuff I've been subjected to. I'm leaving!" and then opens the front door and slams it shut—but does not actually leave.

In some sense the Zionists chose the "wrong" place for their revolution because the place where they chose to defy the past cast them right back to their historical roots. There is thus deep irony in the central role played by the Bible in the early Zionists' rhetoric of national survival and continuity. We could imagine them choosing to ignore the Bible altogether because of its theocentric perspective on history. After all, why continue to identify with a text if you repudiate its central theological message? Yet this is not what happened.

Gershom Scholem correctly identified the profound dialectic within Zionism as the dichotomy between the revolt on the one hand and a desire to continue Jewish history on the other. Continuity and revolt are the essence of the Zionist experience.

> Zionism has never really known itself completely—whether it is a movement of continuation and continuity, or a movement of rebellion. . . . In my opinion it is manifestly obvious that these two trends have determined the essence of Zionism as a living thing with a dialectic of its own, and have also determined all the troubles we are confronted with today. Is Zionism a movement that seeks a continuation of what has been the Jewish tradition throughout the generations, or has it come to introduce a change into the historic phenomenon called Judaism? We all know that when we speak of Judaism we are speaking of something that exists, but which it is difficult to define. Nor is there in my opinion any need to define it. The question is whether we have wanted to alter fundamentally the phenomenon called Judaism, or to continue it. ("Zionism—Dialectic of Continuity and Rebellion," in Ehud Ben Ezer, *Unease in Zion*, p. 273)

In the period following the establishment of the state of Israel, the Bible served as a foundational text for Israeli society. Although religious and secular Zionists had different attitudes toward it, they shared a common passion for it. If you were to ask what the Bible meant to early secular Zionists, the answer would not be "a quest for God." This point is crucial to understanding the contemporary Jewish identity crisis in Israel. The early Zionists looked to the Bible for a new anthropology. They sought in the Bible a different image of the Jew.

Rabbinic and East European Judaism had long presented Jews as the people of the Book. The *talmid hakham* (talmudic scholar), the yeshiva (academy of learning), the intricacies of talmudic legal reasoning—these were the traditional identifications with the ideal Jew. One of the most powerful representatives of the type idealized in traditional Judaism is Rabbi Simeon ben Yohai, who mocked and defied the Romans and consequently was forced into hiding to escape persecution.

For R. Judah, R. Jose, and R. Simeon were sitting, and Judah, a son of proselytes, was sitting near them. R. Judah commenced [the discussion] by observing, "How fine are the works of this people [the Romans]! They have made streets, they have built bridges, they have erected baths." R. Jose was silent. R. Simeon b. Yohai answered and said, "All what they made they made for themselves; they built market-places, to set harlots in them; baths, to rejuvenate themselves; bridges, to levy tolls for them." Now, Judah the son of proselytes went and related their talk, which reached the government. They decreed: Judah, who exalted [us], shall be exalted; Jose, who was silent, shall be exiled to Sepphoris; Simeon, who censured, let him be executed. . . . So they went and hid in a cave. A miracle occurred and a carob-tree and a water well were created for them. They would strip their garments and sit up to their necks in sand. The whole day they studied; when it was time for prayers they robed, covered themselves, prayed, and then put off their garments again, so that they should not wear out. Thus they dwelt twelve years in the cave. Then Elijah came and stood at the entrance to the cave and exclaimed, Who will inform the son of Yohai that the emperor is dead and his decree annulled? So they emerged. . . . R. Phinehas b. Ya'ir his son-in-law heard [thereof] and went out to meet him. He took him into the baths and massaged his flesh. Seeing the clefts in his body he wept and the tears streamed from his eyes. "Woe to me that I see you in such a state!" he cried out. "Happy are you that you see me thus," he retorted, "for if you did not see me in such a state you would not find me thus [learned]." For originally, when R. Simeon b. Yohai raised a difficulty, R. Phinehas b. Ya'ir would give him thirteen answers, whereas subsequently when R. Phinehas b. Ya'ir raised a difficulty, R. Simeon b. Yohai would give him twenty-four answers. (T.B. Sabbath 33b–34a)

Phinehas ben Ya'ir wept when he saw the bruises on Simeon ben Yohai's body, but his teacher reminded him that the condition of the body was unimportant. What was important was the mind, the head, a fact that Simeon ben Yohai showed eloquently by his talmudic brilliance. The image that best captured the great talmudic teacher was of a person whose body was weak, deformed, and covered in sores but whose mind radiated the beauty of its intellectual prowess.

This archetypal image of a head without a body dominated talmudic culture for generations. Zionists, however, turned to the Bible in order to restore the body to Jewish self-understanding. In the Bible the Zionists discovered full-blooded human beings with passion and spontaneity, like David, who was portrayed as the author of the Psalms, the warrior, the king with human appetites. Instead of the rabbinic repudiation of the aesthetic appreciation of nature—"Rabbi Jacob said, He who travels on the road while reviewing what he has learnt and interrupts his study and says: 'How fine is that tree, how fair is that field!' Scripture regards him as if he had committed a grave sin" (Pirkei Avot 3:9)—the Zionists offered a reading of the Song of Songs for its celebration of the beauty of nature and of the human body. Instead of the "four cubits of the Law" and the emphasis on ritual, prayer, and Torah learning, the Bible opened them to a broader vision of community defined by social justice, ethics, and utopian politics. The Bible also anchored them to the land and energized them to discover the beauty of the Hebrew language. The Bible was, as it were, a light that illuminated new ways of living in the world as Jews.

Although the Bible is theocentric, the Zionist pioneers believed that they could ignore this without destroying the book's power to reshape their national and personal identity as Jews. The three pilgrimage festivals of Passover, Shavuot, and Sukkoth, for example, were identified not as commemorations of God's involvement in Israel's history but as festivals celebrating the rhythms of nature and the agricultural seasons. Indeed, Shavuot (Festival of Weeks), which traditionally celebrated the covenant with God and the centrality of mitzvoth (divine commandments), was experienced exclusively as a nature festival celebrating the first fruits.

In the Bible one encountered people fighting wars, interacting with nature, living freely and boldly. In a word, the Bible depicted the heroic age of the Jewish people when Jews were physically strong and vibrant. In order to overcome the anthropology of exile, of the frightened, emaciated, mind-obsessed Jew, Zionists turned to the Bible. There they discovered a new anthropology that gave authenticity to Jews who rejected the stereotypical image of the talmudic student.

In Zionism, for example, the central motif of the holiday of Hanukkah is transferred from the miracle of the cruse of oil that remained lit for eight days to the military prowess of the successful Maccabean revolt. I recall when my family and I took up residence in Israel twenty-eight years ago, I watched a Hanukkah program on Israeli television. I was expecting to hear about the significance of the conflict between Judaism and Hellenism, of Jerusalem versus Athens, of morality and law versus aesthetics—the type of discussions to which I had become accustomed when I lived in the diaspora. I was somewhat shocked to hear an Israeli army general explaining the intricacies of the Maccabees' strategy of surprise attack and analyzing their victory in

terms of brilliant military tactics and sophisticated maneu-
vers. I couldn't help but ask myself: "What happened to *my*
Hanukkah? What happened to the significance of the cruse
of oil that miraculously burnt for eight days and the spiritual rededication of the temple following the Maccabean
victory?" I soon realized that in the reborn state of Israel,
Hanukkah enabled Israelis to define their identities anew, as
modern-day Maccabees. The transformation in perception
created by the Zionists was important for developing new
models for the heroic Israeli Jew.

I have argued that for the secular Zionists, the Bible was
the basis of a new anthropology, not of a new quest for God.
It was not valued as a way of discovering how to live one's
daily life in the presence of God but rather as a way of discovering and legitimating new expressions of Jewish peoplehood. For religious Zionists, however, the Bible had a different meaning. It supported their conviction that there was
religious significance to their return to the Promised Land.
Just as the Bible had provided observant Jews with a frame
of reference to make sense of exile, it now gave meaning to
their return.

Many religious Zionists believed that the return to statehood and national renewal were momentous, religiously
significant historical events. And unlike the Talmud, which
confines itself to brilliant legal discussions, the Bible placed
these events in the larger canvas of history. The Bible, with
its prophetic spirit, located the significance of Jewish history within the larger, universal drama of God's involvement with humanity as a whole.

After the Six-Day War, the feeling of the religious Zionists toward the Bible deepened when the land of the Bible,

the Promised Land, suddenly opened up before them. The "Greater Land of Israel" movement, which opposes yielding sovereignty over the entire Land of Israel, including Judea and Samaria, began in response to the feeling that the Jewish people's long history of waiting was now being vindicated by God, that Jews were living through a redemptive drama—the "onset of our redemption." Torah scholars were moved to write books corroborating this growing sense of anticipation of the approaching footsteps of the Messiah. There was a general feeling that God had returned to the land through Israel's dramatic victory. The Bible prepared and conditioned religious Jews to interpret Israel's return to the land in its full biblical dimensions as a sign that God was returning to reestablish His kingdom in history. They once again asserted the central biblical theme that God's kingdom becomes visible through Israel's triumph over its enemies.

The political relevance of biblical territorial promises seemed natural and obvious to people who felt the immediacy of the Bible in the founding moment of Israel's history. The settlers of Judea and Samaria believed they were being true to the biblical story and the biblical covenant. Territorial compromise meant violating the Jews' messianic role in history and undermining the unfolding biblical drama of Israel's covenantal destiny.

The religious and secular Zionists, then, shared an interest in the Bible for different reasons: one group sought a new anthropology, the other a source for ascribing redemptive significance to the Jewish national renaissance. Today, however, that shared framework of discourse has disappeared and a crisis in Jewish identity is occurring in large part because the Bible has lost its power and relevance for the majority of Israelis. Many in the secular community no longer need the Bible to legitimate their new anthropology. Modern technological culture, television, movies, MTV, the Internet, provide Israeli youth with a sense of confidence in their "normalcy." They are in fact so "normal" that they don't want the Bible to make them feel that being like other people needs justification; rather, they assert that being free, uninhibited, and open to new experiences are legitimate forms of being Israelis. Their identity is established and self-justifying; they do not feel threatened by the Eastern European ghetto identities of their parents and grandparents nor do they feel a need to invoke the Bible to legitimate their participation in the drama of Israel's national rebirth.

The older generation of Israelis loved the Bible. They roamed the land celebrating nature and the Jews' return to the labor of the soil from a biblical perspective. But today that generation is dying, and what had once been the national literature of the country is slowly being discarded as arcane and irrelevant. There may be more Israeli university students studying Eastern religions than majoring in the Bible! The older generations of Zionists are terrified; they see a new generation emerging with no anchorage in Jewish history, and they search for a way to instill their ideological passion in their children.

For the religious Zionist community, the current peace process has destroyed a fundamental part of their religious appreciation of the state of Israel. As they see it, the very fact that you are willing to give up portions of the Promised Land—and the government is prepared to do just that (a prime minister was assassinated by fanatics because of it)—means that you are turning your back on what was supposed to be a redemptive biblical drama. In abandoning the biblical map of Israel you undermine the national will to survive by destroying the biblical significance of your national renaissance. Jews nurtured by this religious outlook desperately need an alternative idea to structure their religious understanding of Israel.

There is a third contributing factor to the present crisis, namely, the militant anti-Zionist religious forces who have deepened the polarization between the religious and the secular Zionists. The image conveyed by this increasingly powerful religious community is based on the paradigm of East European ghetto Jewry. For the ultra-Orthodox haredim, Jewish continuity entails the repudiation of modernity. Their basic claim is that our survival in the past was due to our separation and insulation from the world at large. Therefore, contemporary Jews have two choices: integrate into modern secular society and thus assimilate or return to religious forms of life that reject modernity. These are the only alternatives for the ultra-Orthodox. Consequently, religious and secular Zionists view the ultra-Orthodox haredim with suspicion, hostility, and overt expressions of hatred, feeling that these radicals threaten the Zionist enterprise by advocating a voluntary reghettoization of Jews in modern Israel.

This polarization is more negative and more alarming than the normal conflicts of rival cultural and ethnic traditions within modern pluralistic societies. It is important that we understand the depth of the divisions threatening to destroy Israeli society, schisms that breed such estrangement, contempt, and highly charged, abusive rhetoric that the traditional, spiritually oriented Jerusalem and the modern cosmopolitan Tel Aviv appear to be two separate countries. Some comment ironically that you need a passport to go from one city to the other!

North American Jews have trouble realizing the magnitude of the problem. The popular slogan of the United Jewish Appeal, "We are One," and their conviction that the creation of Israel has united the Jewish people have little to do with the reality of Israeli life. North American Jews may enjoy inspiring rhetoric during their short visits or missions to Israel, but the truth is that Israel hasn't succeeded in bringing unity to the Jewish people. Instead, it has exposed deep divisions and distrust, a fact that one sees clearly in the demonization of the haredim by secular Israelis and of the Conservative and Reform Jews by the religious establishment.

I have attributed the weakening of Jewish historical solidarity among Israeli youth to the loss of the Bible as the foundational text of Israeli society. The crisis in Jewish identity, however, is not only an Israeli phenomenon but represents as well a worldwide dilemma, manifested in the breakdown of traditional Judaism and the growth of Jewish assimilation. Israelis concerned about the growing crisis of assimilation facing diaspora Jewry are losing their faith that the state of Israel will provide a viable secular alternative to the traditional religious forms of Jewish identity.

One of the salient features of modern Jewry is the lack of consensus about what constitutes membership in the Jewish people. The impact of modern history on Jewish life has led to the gradual disintegration of the organizing frameworks which defined the Jewish community both internally, in terms of standards of membership, and externally, in terms of relations with the outside world. The social phenomena associated with this process were the breakdown of the ghetto, the eighteenth-century Haskala (enlightenment), the exposure of Jews to new cultural and religious forms of expression, the rebirth of the Hebrew language in literature and poetry, the flowering of Yiddish culture, and the emergence of Reform and Conservative Judaism. These changes created deep divisions within the community, further exposing Jews to the powerful assimilationist forces of pluralistic secular societies.

It is certainly strange that a people that has existed for three thousand years can continue to ask the question "Who is a Jew?" like a teenager with an identity crisis. The crucial issue of who has the legal authority to determine membership in the community is intimately connected with the question of whether there are *any* necessary conditions for membership. Are there fundamental beliefs and practices that define the community of Israel, or is the willingness to identify with Jews sufficient? The once assumed connection between minimal faith and membership in the Jewish people can no longer be taken for granted with respect to the majority of Jews. The modern experience is marked by a rupture in the Jewish people's understanding of themselves as a Torah covenantal people.

This is not to say that there was always unanimity or that ideological factionalism did not exist in Jewish life in the past. My point, however, is that by and large the divisions that emerged in the past were rationalized and argued from within a common framework, be it the shared legal structure of Halakhah or the language of biblical and rabbinic literature. Differences were often viewed as differences of interpretation. The framework of the Jewish discussion was defined by the covenant with Abraham, the story of the Exodus, the election of Israel, God's revelation of the Torah to the people of Israel, and the rest. The language of both agreement and disagreement was a shared language. The concepts of God, land, covenant, election, and revelation were the building blocks upon which the identity of the community was constructed.

The language of modern Jewish life is far removed from the normative, cultural language that mediated Jewish identity in the past, namely, the discourse of the Torah. Implicit in this discourse was the idea that God had a stake in how one lived one's daily life. A Jew's life mirrored God's authority in the world. The discourse of the Torah, like the discourse of *qedusha* (the holy) and the discourse of mitzvah (divine commandment), is a normative language. A religious life is essentially a disciplined life, an examined life, a life measured against claims and expectations. The modern break with this mode of discourse is evident in the translation of the term *mitzvah* as "good deed" rather than "divine commandment." A good deed is a worthy act, but it lacks any connection with the concept of divine demand.

Traditionally, Jewish identity was affirmed daily through the recital of the *qeri'at shema:* Hear, Israel, the Lord is our God, the Lord is one. The reading of the three Bible chapters (Deut. 6:4–9; 11:13–21; Num. 15:37–41) in the morning and evening (during earlier periods, the Ten Commandments were also included) was a covenant renewal ceremony in which a person accepted the authority of God. The qeri'at shema consisted of two distinct parts. The first section, *qabalat malkhut shamayim* (acceptance of the kingdom of heaven) was immediately followed by *qabalat' ol mitzvot* (acceptance of the yoke of the commandments), the commitment to live according to the mitzvoth of the Torah.

This daily ritual gave expression to the type of person the Jewish tradition wished to cultivate. The qeri'at shema presented the Jew as a commanded one, a participant in a covenantal community. Today, however, this mode of consciousness has disappeared for almost 80 percent of the Jewish people. The problem of modernity revealed in the preoccupation with Jewish identity and continuity reflects this radical shift in the nature of Jewish self-understanding.

For many Jews, three thousand years of Jewish history are no longer considered a framework for their lives. Jewish history is a fact, not a claim. Their connection to the talmudic teacher Rabbi Akiva and to Maimonides places no burden upon Jews nor does it affect their perceptions of how their community ought to live. The break with the consensual frameworks of the past is most apparent in the state of Israel, which offered Jews a new form of Jewish society in which the traditional tacit assumption of the Torah as constitutive of Jewish identity was absent. Jewish national existence in Israel represents a forceful expression of the collective will of a people to continue without the requirement of faith. Loyalty to Jewish history does not entail loyalty to the God of Israel, the Jewish tradition, or the authority of Halakhah. The state thus provides a frame of reference for Jewish membership and community consciousness independent of specific religious content.

Official Israeli policy regarding the law of return is explicit: No commitments of faith are necessary as long as no alternative faith is adopted. A Jew is accepted regardless of whether he or she is atheist, secularist, or completely un-interested in the religious meaning of Jewish life or history. In other words, a Jew wishing to return to Israel cannot seek religious meaning in any faith other than Judaism, but he or she can renounce all faiths including Judaism.

I would argue that this revolution in consciousness is more pronounced in Israel than in the diaspora because of the presence of a viable Jewish social and cultural reality independent of a religious frame of reference. In the dias-pora, the secular dimensions of community have become less effective than in the past and seem to lack the bond-ing qualities required for sustaining Jewish communal life. The synagogue and traditional forms of religious practice provide the primary structures within which Jewish soli-darity and communal identification are expressed. People often join synagogues solely to be part of the larger Jew-ish family. Ritual and religious symbols are the language through which community identification is mediated.

The failure of a secular option for Jewish identification in America stands in sharp contrast with its apparent success in Israel. Israel is the most viable option for Jews who wish to place their Jewish identities within a secular frame of ref-erence. Israel allows Jews to become part of secular Western culture without feeling that they have betrayed the family. In the diaspora, however, the secular alternative still evokes images of turning off the lights on Jewish history. This dis-tinction between Israel and the diaspora must be borne in mind in order to appreciate the factors contributing to the loss of pride and confidence in the secular option of Israeli society.

The significance of Israel as the incarnation of the secular option extends beyond its geographical and political borders. The meaning of the Zionist revolution as understood by Shlomo Avineri, a leading Israeli political scientist, is that even Jews in the diaspora can enjoy a new sense of membership in Jewish history without having to subscribe to a religious interpretation of Jewish nationalism. His argument is that whereas at one time religion kept the Jewish people together, in the modern world its influence has waned and been successfully replaced by new bonds: Israel, the Hebrew language, the mystique of Israel's military capacities, the renewal of the land, and so on. Zionism provides an "Israeli experience" for the Jews of the diaspora, that is, a sense of connection with Jewish history without religious demands or aspirations. "Zionism was the most fundamental revolution in Jewish life. It substituted a secular self-identity of the Jews as a nation for the traditional and Orthodox self-identity in religious terms. It changed a passive, quietistic and pious hope of the return to Zion into an effective social force, moving millions of people to Israel. It transformed a language relegated to mere religious usage into a modern, secular mode of intercourse of a nation state" (Avineri, "Zionism as a Revolution," in *Making of Modern Zionism,* p. 13).

According to Avineri, the new frame of reference for Jewish identity is the state of Israel. With the birth of the nation-state, the traditional religious grounds of Jewish identification that placed Jewish consciousness within an ongoing text-centered interpretive tradition, with being "a nation of priests and a holy nation," were replaced by the secular categories of nationalism and statehood. Avineri's thesis is that the state of Israel has in a sense become a new

Torah for Jews, a substitute for the traditional frame of reference that informed Jewish self-understanding. Zionism transformed Jewish collective consciousness from that of a covenantal people, a singular people whose destiny was to bear witness to the sanctifying power of the Torah in history, to that of just another community among the community of nations (see pp. 217–27).

Avineri's analysis may be less accurate as an empirical description of how most Israelis actually feel than as a provocative thesis of how to view the revolutionary importance of Zionism. His thesis draws attention to the fact that Zionism is undoubtedly one of the most serious ideological challenges to Judaism in modern history. Unlike the social and ideological dangers of Marxism, of assimilation into Western cultures, or of conversions to other faiths, this threat is internal. Secular conceptions of Israeli nationalism call into question the community's traditional understanding of what constitutes a Jew or a Jewish way of life.

The Zionist rationale for supplanting the religious dimension of the Jewish past rests on Zionism's belief in the primacy of the nation as an end in itself rather than a transparent symbol of God's rule in history. However important their role in the past, Torah and Halakhah should not be regarded as essential components of Jewish identity. The concepts of God, election, the call to be a holy people are remnants of an early religious stage of our national consciousness. A Torah way of life should be viewed instrumentally, that is, as a means of national survival, not as a permanent foundation of Jewish identity. This radical reformulation preserves many of the central categories and concerns of Jewish identity—land, peoplehood, history, and language—while offering radically new interpretations of their value and meaning. The framework appears intact, but its content has been transformed from within.

Although secular Zionists have emptied Jewish history of religious content, they nonetheless share with religious Jews a common interest in the continuity of the community as a tangible political and social entity. Zionists fear that the problem of antisemitism will not disappear, and the Jewish people cannot survive through their participation in a religious way of life. The Torah can no longer be the organizing principle of Jewish collective consciousness but should be replaced by the idea of the Jewish nation. The Zionist solution thus involves a fundamental transmutation of values. The tradition defined Israel as God's elect community. Liberation *and* election, the Exodus *and* Sinai were the constitutive moments of the divine drama of Jewish history. Zionism, however, turns Jewish history into a national drama. Instead of theology and the vocabulary of the sacred, it substitutes the language of politics, economics, and social survival to explain the historical destiny of the Jewish people.

The most heated debates over the "Who is a Jew?" issue can often be reduced to two fundamentally irreconcilable conceptions of Jewish history and national consciousness. One position holds that God has an ultimate stake in the everyday behavior of Jews. Israel is unique by virtue of its being a covenantal community, and therefore its history should not be interpreted according to the same rules, laws, and patterns that govern other nations. The opposing view, a basic doctrine of the Zionist revolution, denies all claims that transcend ordinary categories of political analysis, especially providential explanations that set Israel apart from other nations. Israel is a sociopolitical entity like other nations. The language of miracle and providence, of special destiny and divine purpose, is deceptive and must be expunged from our political discourse. The biblical and the rabbinic understandings of Israel are appropriate only as myth and metaphor. Secularization is necessary if Israel is to become responsible for its own destiny.

This cultural revolution struck at the core of the community's identity. The Jewish people were desacrilized into a community whose folkways and rituals no longer expressed an underlying theological and spiritual drama. Traditional symbols and mores were not abolished but rather reinterpreted as instruments of national survival. Rituals are no longer mitzvoth but symbols of Jewish collective existence. As Ahad Ha'am observed: "It is not so much that the Jews kept the Sabbath as that the Sabbath kept the Jews" ("The Sabbath and Zionism," p. 286).

The question of religion in this secular frame of reference is how it can best serve the survival of the Jewish people. In the diaspora too this transformation has taken place. The crucial question diaspora Jews face is not "How do I worship God in the twenty-first century?" but "Will my grandchildren be Jewish?" Their concern is with continuity rather than the need to revive a Torah people. Traditional symbols and institutions such as the synagogue, prayer, or bar and bat mitzvah, and the symbolic language of religious myth and practice, are often solely devices for building a cohesive framework for Jewish survival. The Jewish nation and Israel thereby usurp God's role in defining the meaning and purpose of Jewish history.

Part of the difficulty in grasping the radical nature of the

Zionist revolution is due to the persistence of the concepts of family and peoplehood as the central metaphors of Jewish identity. The notion of peoplehood was always an essential component of traditional Judaism. Unlike many religions, Judaism cannot be explained in terms of faith alone. Its sacred texts deal primarily with the history of a particular people. Consciousness of shared destiny and history are inseparable from faith. "One who separates himself from the community, even if he does not commit a transgression but only holds aloof from the congregation of Israel, does not fulfill religious precepts in common with his people, shows himself indifferent when they are in distress, does not observe their fast, but goes his own way, as if he were one of the gentiles and did not belong to the Jewish people—such a person has no portion in the world to come" (Maimonides, "Laws of Repentance" 3:11).

Consequently, the vitality of these concepts in Israel today often masks the enormity of the change in Jewish consciousness. The situation can be compared to the experience of returning to one's family after a long absence. Despite very real changes and differences, one's memories of familiar faces and places, of the old neighborhood, may combine to produce an overall sense of familiarity that may hide those changes. The sense of family and the symbols of family solidarity which persist in Israel in spite of their changed meaning can deceive us into thinking that a radical rupture has not occurred in Jewish history.

The bold, revolutionary establishment of the Jewish state met with unanticipated historical and cultural setbacks that left the confrontation between the Jewish tradition and modernity unresolved. The fact that the revolution took place in the land of the Bible challenged the new secular Israeli to make sense of his or her connection with the past. Secular Israelis also needed to demonstrate continuity with the past because many segments of their society resisted secularism. The "superiority" of the new revolutionary ideal over the old was not universally acknowledged. Many Israelis remained deeply traditional, refusing the secularization that claimed to be synonymous with modernity. The Sephardic community, for example, presented an ideological challenge to the builders of the new society.

The reality of history intervened and showed the new Israel that it had to learn to live with the old Israel. Had there been no Holocaust and had secularization been allowed to continue its sweep of Europe, there might have been no need to compromise the goals of the revolution with traditional elements. The Holocaust slowed the advance of secularism. The demise of religion and of traditional society had not occurred as expected. The eighteenth-century idea of progress and the belief in the inevitable success of secularization had not been realized. Religious yearning did not disappear from the human spirit. The certainty and single-mindedness of the revolution was thus upset by the failure of secular liberalism to become the exclusive basis of Jewish self-understanding in the twentieth century and by the Holocaust's destruction of the large potential base of a secular aliyah.

Another important source of dissonance for secular Zionism was (and is) Israel's relationship with the diaspora. Those who believe in the radical secular nature of the new Israel are at a loss to explain their relationship with the diaspora upon which Israel relies for economic and political support and as a source of potential aliyah. This interaction also raises questions in the minds of Israelis about their own identities.

Israeli identity has become more ambiguous and complicated because of a confident, thriving diaspora. Diaspora Jews do not perceive themselves only in terms of antisemitism and Jewish vulnerability, a fact that forces Israelis to struggle with forms of Jewish self-consciousness that normalization and statehood were supposed to have resolved. The existence of the diaspora, therefore, has in many ways forced Israelis to reconsider the meaning of their revolution and its connection with and significance for world Jewry.

Jewish cohesion in the diaspora is grounded in religion; what, then, do Israelis have to offer diaspora Jews concerned with continuity? To think only in terms of future aliyah is futile. Jews are not returning en masse to their home in Zion. A permanent diaspora seems to be a perennial condition of Jewish history. The early Zionist doctrine of *shlilat ha-golah* (the negation of the diaspora) continues to be challenged by the existence of a strong diaspora community that values itself as a legitimate framework of Jewish existence and turns to Israel as a significant partner in the Jewish discussion of the relation of Judaism to modernity.

The diaspora is thus extremely important in stimulating Israelis to face the issue of Jewish content in Israeli society. In Israel the "thinness" of meaningful Judaic content in their lives is often buried under the socially comforting reality of being the majority culture, speaking Hebrew, and conforming to the standards of Israeli life. The lack of traditional Jewish content becomes troubling when Israelis go abroad or when they are asked disturbing questions: What do you have to offer the Jews of the world? Does the disappearance of four million Jews through assimilation bother you? What Jewish content can you export? Do you have anything to suggest to Jews not willing to become citizens of the state of Israel whose Jewish identity in the diaspora is voluntary? The belief that Israel should be the organizing framework for Jewish identity throughout the world undermines belief in the viability of a normal secular identity in Israel. To the degree that world Jewish solidarity is a central motif of Israeli culture, the crisis facing diaspora Jewry continues to be a barometer measuring the traditional Jewish content of Israeli society and identity.

It is therefore impossible to escape the issues involved in the confrontation of modernity with the three-thousand-year-old Judaic religious tradition. Can Judaism thrive in a democratic pluralistic society? How can a majority of non-observant Israelis become empowered to reclaim the Jewish tradition without repudiating all that they value in the modern world? How can we provide a religious response to the rebirth of nationhood without placing our national renaissance within the continuum of a redemptive messianic process? Can we respond to events religiously without claiming to know God's will or perceiving Israel in eschatological terms? The categories and language with which we discuss these issues will define the future health and viability of Israeli society.

The growing divisions and animosity between Jews concerned with rituals and traditional symbols of Jewish particularity, on the one hand, and those committed to the liberal values of democracy, human rights, and individual freedom, on the other, threaten the social and political viability of Israeli society. Must the rebirth of nationhood and the concern with security and Jewish survival be antithetical to sharing in a universal language of moral discourse? The perennial Jewish debate regarding universalism versus particularism surfaces repeatedly in the acrimonious political rhetoric of Israeli society.

This book will focus on how the Jewish tradition provides multiple perspectives for dealing with these complex and difficult issues. In chapters two and three, I shall explore the respective philosophical approaches of Yehuda Halevi and Moses Maimonides to revelation, the election of Israel, and the relation between Creation and revelation. Maimonides and Halevi offer two distinct religious sensibilities that can shed light on the conflict between traditional Judaism and modern democratic values. In chapter four, I shall show how the rabbinic tradition focused on the Torah rather than events as the representation of God's presence in history. This shift from a biblical, event-centered theology to a rabbinic, text-centered theology can explain how Maimonides was able to minimize the significance of messianism and to identify the God of the Philosophers with the God of Abraham, Isaac, and Jacob. In the final chapter, I shall argue in favor of using the Sinai covenant rather than messianism to evaluate the religious significance of Israel. I shall also suggest different theological perspectives that can provide a more inclusive and inviting framework for the modern Israeli quest to reengage with Jewish tradition.

# CHAPTER TWO

# The God of History in Yehuda Halevi

Yehuda Halevi and Moses Maimonides were two of the most influential figures in the Jewish philosophical tradition. Both were committed to the centrality of halakhic practice, to revelation, and to the primacy of the talmudic tradition in defining Jewish life. Yet their understandings of Jewish spirituality as mediated and structured by Halakhah and the talmudic tradition were very different.

Although their credentials as committed halakhic Jews are universally acknowledged by practicing members of the Jewish community, the influence of Halevi in shaping modern Orthodox religious sensibilities is far greater than that of Maimonides. In Israel today, for example, religious nationalists regard Halevi rather than Maimonides or other medieval Jewish thinkers as the spiritual precursor of religious Zionism. His great love for the Hebrew language and poetry, his yearning for Zion (which led him, like the rabbi in his ever popular *Kuzari*, to make aliyah), and his interpretation of exile as a national disease, an unnatural condition preventing the full flowering of the spiritual potential of the Jewish people, have contributed to the widespread perception of Halevi as the prototypical philosopher of modern religious Jewry and one of the most beloved spiritual forebears of modern Zionism. Many scholars regard the *Kuzari* as the finest and most authentic expression of the traditional Jewish worldview.

Maimonides, however, evokes mixed reactions among Jewish scholars. On the one hand, they cannot ignore the fact that for the past eight hundred years observant Jews have lived according to his halakhic code, the *Mishneh Torah*. All major codes of Jewish law are rooted in this monumental work. Maimonides is indisputably the master of the rabbinic tradition. In the words of the celebrated saying: "From Moses to Moses [Maimonides], no one has arisen such as Moses."

His unique stature separates Maimonides from other medieval Jewish thinkers; they wrote philosophical works on Judaism but had little or no impact on Jewish practice. This explains the reticence felt by traditional Jews in openly challenging Maimonides' philosophical works or admitting the marginality of his influence on the intellectual and spiritual attitudes of traditional Orthodox communities.

The paradox of Maimonides is that while he, more than any other Jewish philosopher, mediated the halakhic way in which traditional Jews serve God, his theological, spiritual, and psychological views appear to undermine the very beliefs and religious attitudes that traditional Jews regard as sacred. This is the reason for the perennial fascination with Maimonides: how is it that the person who was responsible for shaping the structure and ethos of Jewish normative practice was committed to a conception of God, history, and philosophy that, to many, threatened its very foundations?

My comparison of Halevi and Maimonides will predominantly draw upon their respective classics of Jewish thought, the *Kuzari* and the *Guide of the Perplexed,* and will focus on their distinctive approaches to the tensions between reason and revelation, nature and history, the "God of the Philosophers" and the "God of Abraham, Isaac, and Jacob."

In the *Kuzari,* the juxtaposition of the rabbi's statement of belief in "the God of Abraham, Isaac, and Jacob" and the king's rejoinder: "Why did you not refer to God as the Creator of heaven and earth?" is the best starting point for distinguishing between the religious outlooks of Maimonides and Halevi. Much depends on whether the controlling metaphor or idea that shapes one's spiritual universe is drawn from nature and the cosmos or from within the bounds of history. The literary and intellectual structure of the *Kuzari* locates Jewish thought within a polemical context. Halevi uses the dramatic device of a confrontation of Judaism with Christianity, Islam, and philosophy to defend his conception of Judaism. He sets the plot in motion by introducing an important political and religious figure, the king of the Khazars, who has a disturbing dream in which an angel appears to him and says: "Your way of thinking is indeed pleasing to the Creator, but not your way of acting." As a priest and religious person deeply concerned with the meaning and value of religious life and practice, the king becomes troubled by this expression of divine displeasure. Driven by religious anxiety, he decides to invite a philosopher, a Christian theologian, and a Muslim theologian to explore the meaning of his disturbing dream.

The philosopher's response to the king's dream differs from those of the theologians in that he chooses to ignore the question of divine displeasure and claims instead that God is indifferent to how human beings conduct their religious lives. The ultimate goal of a spiritual life inspired by philosophy is knowledge of the true nature of reality and divinity. The worldview that informed medieval Aristotelianism had no place for a God who was interested, let alone involved, in human affairs. The God of Aristotle was indifferent to history and the affairs of human beings. "Likewise, according to the philosophers, He is beyond the knowledge of particulars because they change with the times, whereas there is no change in God's knowledge. Therefore, He is not aware of you, let alone of your intentions and your actions, nor does He hear your prayer[s] or observe your movements" (*Kuzari* 1:1).

The way of life associated with a philosophical worldview focuses on building moral character and virtuous dispositions aimed at minimizing the distracting influences of the body upon the mind, thereby freeing the mind to become illuminated by the "Active Intellect." The underlying ideal that energizes this form of spirituality is the human quest for knowledge of God and the world. The philosopher is not interested in such questions as Does God answer my prayers? Is God concerned with human suffering? or Is there a divine scheme for history? On the contrary, the philosopher longs to move beyond history, to be free of social, political, and economic concerns in order to become wholly engaged in philosophical reflection.

As far as the philosopher is concerned, the king is free to choose whatever religion he wishes for reasons of convenience, utility, or some other practical advantage. Whether he chose a philosophical form of religious behavior or a more cult-oriented, popular form makes no significant difference. Organized religion has nothing to do with the ultimate telos of human existence and therefore can be chosen on the basis of pragmatic and utilitarian considerations.

Although moved by the persuasive power of the philosopher's understanding of the spiritual life, the king nevertheless found it unsatisfactory.

> The Khazar said to him. Your statement is certainly persuasive, but it is not in keeping with my request because I know by myself that my soul is pure [and that I] direct [my] actions towards pleasing the Lord. Nevertheless, I was told that these actions are not pleasing, even though the intention is pleasing. Undoubtedly, therefore, there are certain actions which are pleasing in themselves [and] not dependent on mere opinions. Otherwise, [consider the fact] that the Christians and the Muslims, who have divided up the [whole] world between themselves, wage war against one another, although each of them has already directed his intention sincerely towards [pleasing] God. (*Kuzari* 1:2)

The king feels compelled to challenge the philosopher's position as failing to account for some of the stubborn facts of religious life; he argues, in effect: If what you say is correct, why then do Christians and Muslims fight one another while serving their own God with pure intention? If practice is not of ultimate importance, what then is the driving force behind the tragic history of religious warfare and bloodshed?

The philosopher's answer—"The philosophers' creed knows no manslaughter, as they only cultivate the intellect"—shows the absurdity and danger of Christians and Muslims attributing ultimate significance to ritual or of the king doing so through his dream. In cultivating a spiritual life that aims at philosophical contemplation and the building of moral character, one avoids the risks of waging holy wars and killing in the name of God.

The argument Halevi puts into the mouth of the king is that a valid theory of religious life must explain why people do, in fact, take religious rituals and practices seriously. The philosopher's account of religion is inconsistent with the sociology of religion and fails as an explanation of how religious communities and cultures live. The history of Christianity and Islam clearly points to the primacy of ritual practice in religious life. This fact can hardly be accommodated by the kind of utilitarian civic religion the philosopher offers. The king thus turns to the Christian and Islamic theologians to join the discussion.

It is here that the king mentions for the first time why he has not invited a rabbi to join the debate. "I will ask the Christians and the Muslims, for undoubtedly one of the two ways of acting is the pleasing one. As for the Jews, well, what is obvious from their despicable condition and paltry numbers, as well as everyone's loathing for them[,] is quite sufficient [for me to ignore them]" (*Kuzari* 1:4).

The Jews are discounted (and this too is a central theme in the *Kuzari*) because of their small number, their hard-

ships, and their powerlessness. Israel's exile and debased
political condition in history were considered valid reasons
for ignoring Judaism. For Halevi one of the most disturbing issues was the powerlessness and insignificance of the
Jewish people in twelfth-century Spain. Islam and Christianity appeared to have preempted the drama of history,
while Jews became marginal and inconsequential. The ines-
capable dilemma facing Jews was how to reconcile the biblical story, which conceived of Jews as God's elect, with the
painful evidence of their weakness and vulnerability. The
basic challenge confronting a concerned Jewish thinker like
Halevi was how to rehabilitate the dignity of his national
community. How do you present a philosophy of exile so
that Jews would not view themselves as historical indigents
and ciphers but would believe in themselves again as a major
force in history?

When the representatives of Christianity and Islam begin to speak, they introduce the biblical themes of creation,
miracles, and divine providence and involvement in human
history into the discussion. When asked by the king about
the source of these doctrines and beliefs, each refers to the
Bible or to what Christians call the Old Testament. The king
quickly realizes that there is an authoritative source of truth
underlying the religious concepts and claims of these two
powerful religious traditions. His search has led him back to
Judaism because Christianity and Islam derive their understandings of miracles and a personal God from the Hebrew
Bible. The king therefore decides to invite a rabbi to join the
discussion and to give Judaism a serious hearing.

What is interesting about the argument concerning the
common roots of Christianity and Islam in the Hebrew

Bible, which is a central theme of the *Kuzari*, is that contrary to the then-prevailing opinion, Judaism has not been an ineffectual force in history. In fact, its influence has been enormous. It provides the foundation on which Christianity and Islam are built. Christianity and Islam are different transmutations of Judaism because their basic religious worldviews are grounded in the Jewish story.

Both Halevi in the *Kuzari* and Maimonides in the "Laws of Kings" in the *Mishneh Torah* treat Christianity and Islam as instruments serving the ultimate triumph and vindication of Judaism. In this way, they reverse the thrust of the generally accepted medieval polemical framework that placed the major monotheistic faiths along a continuum that began with Judaism and ended with either Christianity or Islam. The historical exilic degradation of Israel and the successes of its main rivals were seen as confirming this progression away from Judaism.

According to Halevi, Christianity and Islam fulfill two primary functions that ultimately serve the true interests of Judaism. First, they establish the basic structure of religious life based on religious behavior and grounded in divine revelation; thus they counteract the philosophical prejudice against the idea that God is involved in human history. The intellectual plausibility of Judaism was enhanced by the success of Christianity and Islam in that they contributed to the worldwide acceptance of the idea of revelation as an essential component of religious life. Second, notwithstanding Israel's exilic powerlessness in history and the hostility of Christianity and Islam toward Judaism, Christianity and Islam actually facilitate the eventual messianic triumph of Judaism in history.

Besides, God has a secret with regard to us and a [kind of] wisdom like the wisdom in the seed that falls into the ground. It changes and is transformed in its outward appearance into earth, water, and manure. No perceptible trace of it remains based on what someone who [merely] looks at it would suppose. But, lo and behold! It is what transforms the earth and water into [something having] its own nature, carries them stage by stage to the point [at which] the elements become refined, and turns them into something like itself. It casts off husks, leaves, and other such things so that, when the kernel has become pure and suitable for that divine order to dwell in it as well as the form of the first seed, that tree will bear fruit like the fruit from which its seed was [derived]. So it is with the religion of Moses. All those who come after it are in reality being transformed into it, even though they outwardly reject it. Therefore, these religious communities [that is, the Christians and the Muslims] are only a preparation and prelude to the awaited *Messiah,* who is the fruit [of this process]. All of them will come to be his fruit when they acknowledge him, and the tree will also become one. At that time, they will recognize the excellence of the root that they used to disdain, and [it will be] just as we have said with regard to [the passage], "Indeed, My servant shall prosper" (Isa. 52:13). (*Kuzari* 4:23)

Leo Strauss, in his article "The Law of Reason in the *Kuzari,*" poses the question of why Halevi did not stage a direct discussion between the rabbi and the philosopher. The king engages the rabbi and the philosopher in discussion individually, never together. Strauss explains this in terms of Halevi's belief in the basic incompatibility of Judaism and philosophy. By contrast, the king has a natural affinity for revealed religion, a prerequisite which accounts for his interest in and eventual conversion to Judaism. The *Kuzari* assumes, says Strauss, that the philosopher can never embrace Judaism because the basic presuppositions of a philosophical worldview are wholly at odds with those of revealed religion. The king, on the other hand, is from the start a candidate for conversion by virtue of his personal history and psychological predilections. His natural predisposition is shown by his having served as a priest and, most important, by his dreams and anxieties about whether God is pleased with his religious practices. Since Halevi believed in the radical incompatibility of philosophy and revealed religion, there was no point in even imagining a direct confrontation between the rabbi and the philosopher.

Notwithstanding the plausibility of Strauss's observation, I wish to offer an alternate response to the question he raised. The reason for placing the defense of Judaism within the context of a rabbi's discussion with a king rather than with a philosopher is that the *Kuzari* is primarily concerned with Judaism and the Jewish people as effective forces in history. Halevi's frame of reference is not the cultural and religious struggles of the individual caught between competing truth claims and sensibilities but the meaning and direction of history. This perspective informs both the content and the structure of the *Kuzari*. The dramatic effect of the king's conversion to Judaism attests to the great potential power of Judaism in history.

The *Kuzari* affirms the belief that Israel, even in exile, continues to be the carrier of God's redemptive plan. The successes of Christianity and Islam are themselves signs of the hidden power of Israel in shaping the future of history. This perspective sheds light on the rabbi's decision to depart for the Land of Israel. This act of faith in the face of harsh political realities gave further expression to the underlying theme of the *Kuzari*, namely, that the Jewish people are not dead, a relic of the past.

Halevi, like his counterpart in the *Kuzari*, demonstrated his belief in God's miraculous redemptive power by leaving the diaspora and embarking on a journey to the Promised Land. This bold act expressed Halevi's deep trust in the abiding grace of God. Halevi was not deterred by the fact that the political realities of his time relegated the Jews to a minor role in comparison with those of the two major protagonists, the Crusaders and the Muslims, in the struggle to control the Holy Land. Political realism and pragmatism aside, Halevi believed that the history of Israel could not be explained in the same empirical causal terms that were appropriate for other nations.

Halevi's solution was that redemption would become a reality if, and only if, Israel returned to its land and lived in accordance with the mitzvoth revealed to Moses at Sinai. Observance of the mitzvoth in the Land of Israel would transform the Jews into genuine messengers of the living God. The only requirement was that they take their faith seriously. The Jewish people's return to the land was a crucial condition for the return of prophecy and for the unfolding of Israel's unique spiritual capacities.

The works of Jewish philosophers often contain exegesis of key passages in the biblical narrative which furnish the main concepts, symbols, and metaphors of Jewish experience, and the works of Halevi and Maimonides are no exception. I shall now look at how these two thinkers interpret and use the same terms and symbols, an illuminating way to highlight the different sensibilities that inform their respective philosophical positions.

A classic example is their different interpretations for the story of the burning bush and specifically God's revelation of His name to Moses as " 'Ehyeh 'asher 'ehyeh" (Exod. 3:14). How a philosopher interprets this enigmatic phrase often reflects the primary theological metaphor that underlies his religious outlook and understanding of Judaism. The difference between Maimonides' and Halevi's interpretations is a clear case in point.

Maimonides translates " 'ehyeh 'asher 'ehyeh" as "I am that I am." I am the being whose existence is not contingent on anything. This principle of absolute self-sufficiency is the central principle of divinity and captures the essential spirit and meaning of the God of the Philosophers. As I shall show in more detail below, Maimonides tried to educate Jews to conceive of God independent of human history and anthropomorphic imagery. Neither revelation nor redemption is necessary to his understanding of divinity. For Maimonides, existence itself was a transparent symbol of divinity. Nature and being per se and not the traditions of a particular community or history create certainty about divine existence.

Halevi's approach was diametrically opposed to Maimonides'. Nature cannot provide grounds of certainty about divinity equal to those of the lived history of Israel. *"'Ehyeh 'Asher 'Ehyeh"* should be understood as I will be present for you in the future as I have been present in the past. God answers Moses: I am "the One who is present, who will be present with you when you seek Me. So, let them not seek any greater proof [of My true reality] than My being found together with them" (*Kuzari* 4:3).

For Halevi, the history of Israel makes the divine reality accessible to human beings. The triumphant story of the exodus from Egypt and the spectacular miracles performed in the desert demonstrate the reality of the living God. In the

*Kuzari,* therefore, when the king questions the rabbi about his belief, the latter answers: "I believe in the God of Abraham, Isaac and Israel, who brought the children of Israel out of Egypt with signs and miracles." When the king responds by asking, "Should you not have said that you believe in the Creator of the world, its Governor and Guide?" the rabbi answers that belief in God based on the testimony of nature and rational argument is susceptible to uncertainty and doubt, whereas the testimony of the patriarchs guarantees certainty because they personally experienced God's miraculous presence. This answer, says the rabbi, is the essence of the biblical message:

> Moses began addressing Pharaoh in the same way too, when he told him "The God of the Hebrews has sent me to you," meaning, the God of Abraham, Isaac and Jacob, since their story was well-known among the nations as well as [the fact] that a divine order accompanied them, took interest in them, and performed wonders for them. He did not tell him, "the Lord of heaven and earth," or "my Creator and your Creator sent me." And God also began His address to the multitude of the children of Israel in the same way [by saying], "I am [the] God, whom you worship, who brought you out of the land of Egypt. . . ." He did not say, "I am the Creator of the world and your Creator." Accordingly, I began [to speak to] you this way, O commander of the Khazars, when you asked me about my faith. I answered you in terms of what is compelling for me and for the community of the children of Israel for whom that [which I have described] is well established on the basis of direct observation and subsequently, through uninterrupted tradition, which is as valid as direct observation. (*Kuzari* 1:25)

The Exodus is a cornerstone of Israel's belief in the reality of God. Only through the history of Israel is there access to the living God. Since later generations did not participate in the founding experiences of God's providential involvement in Israel's early history, traditional communities of faith must not only transmit reliable information about the past, but they must also create conditions for reliving and reexperiencing the original moments of God's manifestation in history. Their narratives must be plausible, but they must also be vivid and engaging. It is for this reason that the Exodus from Egypt, the desert experience, and the revelation at Sinai are preserved and transmitted with all their dramatic force and vitality.

The creation of the world, according to the *Kuzari,* was the source of the Jews' unique spiritual capacity, which explains God's providential relationship to the people of Israel. When creating Adam, God instilled in him and some of his descendants an attribute, which Halevi calls *'amr 'ilahi,* that is not universally shared by human beings (see Pines, "Shi'ite Terms and Conceptions in Judah Halevi's *Kuzari*"). Unlike the common properties of human nature, this divine capacity was transmitted selectively through the line of Seth, through Noah to Abraham, Isaac, and Jacob, and then to all Jacob's descendants (*Kuzari* 1:95). To realize this inherited potentiality, the people of Israel must live in accordance with the rules of the Torah revealed by God at Sinai. Creation thus begins a process that culminates in the revelation of the Torah. The Jews are worthy of receiving revelation because they alone are the true descendants of Adam and the inheritors of the spiritual capacity that God bequeathed to him.

According to Halevi, communion with God cannot be achieved through human reasoning. "In the worship of God, there is no supposing, nor speculating, nor judging on one's own. If this were the case, the philosophers would have attained by means of their sciences and intellects many times more than what the children of Israel attained" (*Kuzari* 1:99).

God's covenantal relationship with Israel points to Israel's unique religious capacity. A Torah way of life is, as it were, sui generis. Its source and development are separate from the normal framework of human development. Halevi's understanding of creation explains the necessity and urgency of revelation. For the philosopher, the power that drives the spiritual quest for communion with God lies within the rational capacities of human beings. For Halevi, intellectual curiosity cannot nurture and satisfy our spiritual longings because only revelation can provide the certainty of being on the right path to God. Revelation is not a shortcut or a supplement to the truths the philosopher discovers through a lengthy process of critical reflection; it is the source of unique and radically distinct content not discoverable by human intellectual efforts. Halevi offers a strong argument in support of the indispensability of revelation.

The anthropology described by the philosophers equates human self-realization with intellectual perfection, that is, with gaining knowledge of reality and contemplating the truths of being. Halevi's anthropology draws a sharp distinction between the natural and the spiritual. A religious anthropology, according to Halevi, postulates spiritual needs that cannot be nurtured by the intellect but only by following the way of life prescribed by revelation. According to Halevi's understanding of Creation, God distinguished human beings from animals by the rational faculty, which was given to all human beings, and by a special spiritual faculty instilled in certain human beings which enabled them to achieve prophecy. The fullest realization of this special capacity required specific conditions that only prophetic knowledge can provide.

> The meaning of *Elohim* may be grasped by reasoning because the intellect leads to [the conclusion] that the world has a Ruler and source of order. People differ about it in accordance with their ways of reasoning, but the most important of the opinions about Him is that of the philosophers. As for the meaning of *YHWH*, it cannot be grasped by reasoning, but rather by being witnessed in that prophetic [kind of] seeing by which man is almost able to separate himself from his species and attach himself to an angelic species so that a *different spirit* (Num. 14:24) arises within him, just as it says, "You will become another man" (1 Sam. 10:6). ... Then, the aforementioned doubts, which used to fill one with misgivings about *Elohim[,]* will be resolved for man, and he will make light of [all] those syllogistic arguments that are used to acquire knowledge of [His] lordship and unity. (*Kuzari* 4:15)

One of the most striking differences between Maimonides' approach (which I shall discuss in the next chapter) and Halevi's can be seen in their respective descriptions of Abraham. Abraham as portrayed in the *Kuzari* was initially a philosopher, but after his direct personal experience of God, he turned away from philosophy and the study of nature.

> The Sage said: Well, [then, by that standard] it was right for *Abraham* to have undergone all that he did in *Ur of the Chaldees,* and then in departing from [his] homeland, and also in [accepting] *circumcision,* and again in expelling *Ishmael,* and even further in [his] anxiety about slaughtering *Isaac,* since all that he experienced with respect to the divine order (*al-amr al-ilahi*) he ex-

perienced by "savoring," not by reasoning. Moreover, he saw that nothing relating to his particular circumstances was hidden from Him. He saw too, that [God] rewarded him for his goodness moment by moment and also guided him towards His righteous paths so that [Abraham] would neither go forwards nor backwards unless it was with His authorization. How, then, could he not look down upon his earlier syllogistic arguments? Thus, [it was] just as the *Sages, of blessed memory,* explained homiletically with regard to [the verse], *He took him* outside (Gen. 15:5). *[God] said to him: Abandon your astronomy* (Shabbat, 156a: Nedarim 32b). It means that He ordered him to abstain from his [preoccupation with the] sciences based on reasoning, such as astronomy and other [such] things, and to take upon himself the duty of obeying the One he had experienced by way of tasting, just as it says, *Savor and see how good YHWH* is (Ps. 34:9). Thus, YHWH is rightly called the *God of Israel,* (Ex. 5:1) because this outlook (*nazar*) [on God] is entirely lacking among other [peoples] beside[s] themselves. (*Kuzari* 4:17)

Abraham's earlier knowledge of the structure of nature and metaphysics could not mediate God's presence for him once he experienced the immediacy of divinity. He could no longer be satisfied with merely contemplating God after he experienced the richness of living with God. He now felt passion, love, joy, and an intimacy of relationship that claimed his whole being, not just his intellect. By comparison, his earlier form of philosophical spirituality was emotionally truncated and barren, for it lacked the basic ingredients necessary for achieving spiritual communion with God.

Moreover, at that time man will become a [true] worshiper, passionately in love with the One he worships, [ready to] perish for the sake of His love because of the tremendous joy he finds in being attached {to Him} as well as the hurt and loss [he feels] in being far from Him. [This is] in direct contrast to those who de-

vote themselves to philosophy, who see in the worship of God
{only} good manners and a statement of what is true with reference to His being exalted above [all] other things that exist, just
as the sun ought to be exalted above [all] other things that are
visible, and [who maintain] that there is nothing more involved in
the denial of God than a [certain] baseness of soul that is content
to accept falsehood. (*Kuzari* 4:15)

For Halevi, *qiddush ha-shem* (sanctification of God's
name, martyrdom) points to an important difference between revealed and philosophical religions. The absence of
martyrdom in philosophical religion is a sign of its failure
to create the same devotion and passion as revealed religion.
Why should the philosopher (as described by Halevi) be
expected to give up his life for his beliefs? Whereas Abraham's faith was driven by a love of God which claimed him
totally, the philosopher's attachment to God is fundamentally a matter of knowledge. Worshiping false gods is, according to the philosopher's credo, equivalent to making
an intellectual error. It is no wonder, then, that martyrdom
is almost exclusively connected with revealed religion and
rarely, if ever, with philosophic religion.

The Khazar said: The difference between *Elohim* and *YHWH* has
now become clear to me, and I have also understood the difference between the *God of Abraham* and the *God of Aristotle.* One
longs for *YHWH, exalted be He,* by way of tasting and witnessing
for oneself whereas one inclines towards *Elohim* by way of reasoning. Moreover, that [same] tasting calls upon the one who has
experienced it to give [his] all for the sake of His love and even
[to prefer] death [to living] without Him whereas this [same] reasoning makes one see that giving Him pre-eminence is obligatory
whenever there is no harm [involved in doing so] and one does
not undergo hardship because of it. (*Kuzari* 4:16)

A philosophical, naturalistic approach to God can provide the basis for institutionalized community religion but only so far as it justifies "civic religion"—the minimal ethical and social norms required for maintaining social order and peace. Philosophical religion is not necessarily devoid of ritual and symbol. The crucial difference between philosophical and revealed religions lies in the former's naturalistic psychology, which confines the spiritual dimension of life to reason alone, while revealed religion distinguishes the direct experience of God with the philosophical contemplation of God. Halevi believed that religious practices that often appear bizarre and unintelligible in the light of natural reason become understandable and even indispensable after we witness their efficacy and transforming effects. Halevi draws the following striking analogy to clarify his argument.

> [It is] as if you had never heard of sexual intercourse and were not acquainted either with it or its outcome, but you see yourself lusting after a woman's vilest organ; and you realize what vileness is [involved] in getting intimate with her and also what baseness there is in submitting to the woman. You would surely be amazed, and you would say, "These movements are simply useless and mad!" until [the time came] when you saw someone like yourself emerge from a woman. The [whole] thing would amaze you, and you would imagine that you were among those assisting in the [baby's] creation and that the Creator intended to have this world built up through you. It is the same with the actions [prescribed by] the religious Law, which are determined by God, exalted be He. You slaughter the sheep, for example, and get soiled by its blood, and also by skinning it, cleansing its intestines, washing it thoroughly, dismembering it, sprinkling its blood [on the altar], putting the firewood for it in order, kindling the fire, and arranging it [all] in tiers. (Lev. 1:3-9) Now if this had not been [done] at God's command (*amr Allahi*) you would surely

have belittled these practices and regarded them as something that [only] distances one from God, exalted be He, not as something [that brings one] close. [But,] eventually, when it has been completed in the proper way, and you see the heavenly fire or discover another spirit within yourself, which you did not know [beforehand], or [you witness] veridical dreams and miracles, you know that they are the result of all that you did before and of the mighty order with which you have come into contact and which you have [now actually] attained. (*Kuzari* 3:53)

It is not surprising that the mitzvoth chosen by Halevi to represent the essence of revelation were not *mishpatim* (social and ethical laws) but *huqqim* (ceremonial practices and rituals). Revelation is not necessary in order to justify obeying mishpatim. Even a band of robbers can understand the necessity for minimal social and ethical norms without which the most basic forms of social life would collapse (*Kuzari* 2:48; compare Plato's *Republic* 351C). The essence of Jewish law, therefore, lies not in its social and ethical legislation but rather in its huqqim, laws which logically presuppose revelation, that is, laws that are binding only because they were given by God.

Two biblical collections of norms are of special interest to Halevi: the laws for building the sanctuary in the book of Exodus, and the sacrificial cult described in Leviticus. Like the mystics, Halevi was fascinated with every detail connected with the construction of the sanctuary as well as with the specifics of the sacrificial service: the choice of animals, their mode of slaughter, the treatment of the blood, the entrails, the organs.

The nonrational ritual practices of Judaism, such as the *qorbanot* (sacrifices), are for Halevi paradigms of revealed religion. The elaborate and arcane structure of the laws in the book of Leviticus indicates how far removed spirituality is from rational understanding. Their ultimate and only justification is that God prescribed them and therefore they actually work. These practices make a real difference. Their performance is cathartic and spiritually energizing. The difference between philosophical and revealed religions is dramatically described in Halevi's description of the importance of conforming strictly to all the details of revelation. Purity of heart and inwardness are not sufficient to endow an act with religious significance and cannot provide communion with God.

> {For, in fact,} the descriptions of the sacrifices, and how they are to be offered, in what place, in what direction, how they are to be slaughtered, and how their blood and limbs are to be treated in relation to different arts [were] all [accompanied] by clear explanation from God lest the slightest thing be missing from them, because [if anything were missing] the whole process would be corrupted, just like natural things, which are comprised of minute relations [between things], too minute for the imaginative powers of our minds [to grasp]. If their relations were to be disturbed in the slightest way, then the very thing that was being generated would be corrupted; and then, that plant or animal or limb, for example, would be corrupted too or deprived [of its existence altogether]. (*Kuzari* 1:99)

Halevi compares the person who attempts to seek communion with God through human initiative independent of revelation to a "fool who entered the pharmacy of a physician [who was] well known for his effective medicines. The physician wasn't there, but people would come to that pharmacy seeking help [anyway]. The fool [in turn] would dispense [the contents] of the vials to them without knowing the medicines [they contained] nor even how much {of each} medicine should be dispensed to each individual. Therefore, he killed people by means of the very medicines that might have helped them" (*Kuzari* 1:79).

Just as it is foolish and dangerous to take medicines prepared by sincere, well-meaning people with no knowledge of pharmacology, so too it is foolish and dangerous to trust natural wisdom instead of the "spiritual pharmacology" of revelation in choosing which religious practices to follow. Natural wisdom may get it right sometimes, but in the majority of cases it will miss the mark entirely. There are correct prescriptions for energizing human spirituality and these prescriptions are available from only one source: God's revelation. There is no point in placing one's trust in spontaneity and subjective passion when the prescriptions prepared by the divine pharmacologist were given to us at Sinai. For Halevi "getting it wrong" in any minute way is as catastrophic in religion as it is in nature. Halevi conveys a sense of terror in the notion of a person attempting to approach God independent of revelation. His analogy of this act with the deformities of nature and the danger of being poisoned by an untrained pharmacist make the details of Leviticus paradigmatic of how one should approach Jewish normative practice.

The biblical account of the death of the two sons of Aaron for bringing a "strange fire" into the sanctuary mirrors Halevi's understanding of the danger of introducing new forms of worship into the normative framework of Halakhah. The correct way to God is not determined by the purity of intention and subjective passion but by the precise rules and practices revealed by God. Getting the details wrong can be catastrophic for like the sons of Aaron, one can be "consumed by fire" despite the purity of one's intentions.

This perspective is also the basis of Halevi's interpretation of the sin of the Golden Calf. The king refers to this idolatrous episode ("What sin could be greater than this?"), which appears to cast doubt on the unique spiritual excellence of the people of Israel. Halevi, however, absorbs the incident into his theory of mitzvoth by explaining it as a presumptuous reliance on human initiative independent of revelation. The Calf per se was not the problem since, after all, bulls and cherubim were often used as cultic symbols. The crux of the sin lay in acting independent of the word of God, performing a cultic act that had not been preceded by the words "Thus sayeth the Lord" (see *Kuzari* 1:97).

The sanctuary and the sacrifices constitute the way to God because—and only because—God communicated them. The mitzvoth that nurture Jewish spirituality are, like their revelatory source, discontinuous with the universal canons of human intelligibility. Similarly, the Jewish people's acknowledgment of and commitment to Halakhah are the product not of natural reason but of a special genius that enables them to recognize and be nurtured by this unique way of life. It is no wonder, then, that the sign of the covenant is circumcision, an act with no utility or rational significance. To enter into the covenant is to commit oneself to spiritual values and practices that defy rational explanation. Human rationality must be transcended for Jews to become a covenantal community.

The *Kuzari* ends with the rabbi—the author—going to the land of Israel. This should not be viewed as a prototypical Zionist act but rather as the act of a mystic drawn to the Holy Land, whose soil alone is capable of cultivating the spiritual potential with which Israel is endowed. For Halevi, history will change when Israel becomes capable of channeling its special divine gift into the world. The politics of Israel can never be normal because Israel is not a normal people. Its destiny is not like that of ordinary peoples and cultures.

For Halevi, Israel's history is discontinuous with world history. In contrast to Maimonides, there is, so to speak, no way for "the vertical" to be translated into "the horizontal." The vertical—the human connection with the divine reality—is nontranslatable. As argued earlier, Halevi's idea of revelation absorbs his idea of creation. Ultimately, it is the supreme act of grace, God's giving the special divine power to Adam and, in turn, to all of Israel. Election is closely linked to this notion of creation. Conceptually, election can be said to precede creation, for it is the particularity of divine revelation in history that informs creation by making it the source of Israel's particular spiritual capacity.

For Halevi, the election of Israel is ontologically grounded. The people of Israel in the Land of Israel are alone capable of achieving prophecy. Without the revelatory grace of God and the trustworthiness of the transmitters of God's revelation one cannot approach and understand the God of Israel.

> There is no [way of] coming close to God except by [fulfilling] God's ordinances, exalted be He; and there is no way to the knowledge of God's ordinances, except by way of prophecy, not by means of reasoning with one another and engaging in intellectual speculation. There is no connection between us and those ordinances [revealed to the prophets], except by means of reliable

tradition. Moreover, those who have transmitted those laws to us were not just unique individuals, but rather a great many people [consisting of] scholars, people of stature, and [others] who had contact with the prophets. (*Kuzari* 3:53)

The king in the *Kuzari* is puzzled by the zeal, enthusiasm, and subjective religious passion of the Karaites, who reject the rabbinic tradition despite the rabbi's argument for its indispensability to revelation. Halevi offers a way of understanding the zeal of the Karaites, as well as the laxity and complacency found among followers of the rabbinic tradition, in the following parable.

> The sage said: This relates to what I told you about engaging in intellectual speculation and arbitrary judgment. Those who engage in intellectual speculation about worship pertaining to the *work of heaven* (Jer. 7:18; 44:17) exert themselves [far] more than *someone who does the work of YHWH* (Jer. 48:10) that he is commanded [to do]. For the latter have found rest in their acceptance of tradition on faith, and their souls are tranquil, like someone who goes about freely within the city, without having to be on the alert for any challenge, while the former are like someone who goes about on foot in the desert, who doesn't know what he will meet up with. Therefore, he is armed, alert for battle, schooled in combat, [and] accustomed to it. So don't be surprised by what you see of their resoluteness, and don't be caught off guard by whatever laxity you see on the part of those subject to tradition, I mean, [of course,] the Rabbanites. The former sought out a fortress in which they might be secure, while the latter are asleep, lying quietly on their bedding, in an ancient, [well-]fortified city. (*Kuzari* 3: 37)

Those who live by and practice Judaism in the spirit of Yehuda Halevi find security and comfort in believing that they alone possess the one true way to worship God. They can allow themselves the luxury of observing the mitzvoth with complacency because of their certainty that their way of worship is pleasing to God. Those who must rely on human rational arguments to order their religious lives are exposed to uncertainty, doubt, and confusion and are driven to compensate for that uncertainty by an excess of religious zeal. They cannot go to sleep with the peace of mind that their way of acting is pleasing to God.

# CHAPTER THREE

# The Cosmic God in Maimonides

Many scholars have found great difficulty explaining how the same person could have written the *Mishneh Torah,* Maimonides' code of Jewish law, and the *Guide of the Perplexed,* his main philosophical work. The historian of Jewish philosophy Isaac Husik wrote that "Maimonides did not write his philosophy for the masses, nor did he compose his *Guide of the Perplexed* for the simple and the pious, though learned, students of the Talmud and the other rabbinic literature. They were satisfied with their simple faith, and Maimonides was not interested in disturbing it. For them he composed his *Yad ha-Hazaqah,* the code of the rabbinic law" ("Philosophy of Maimonides," p. 4).

Husik believes that in the *Guide* Maimonides shows his true self, that is, his Aristotelian bent. The theoretical interests of Maimonides, however, run into conflict when he tries to apply Aristotelianism to specific Jewish concerns. The

Torah, with its emphasis on the way an individual acts before God, cannot be integrated with a conception of the world that deals with the development of theoretical perfection. Husik marvels that Maimonides did not recognize the fundamental incompatibility between Aristotelianism and the Torah.

> Maimonides is an Aristotelian and he endeavors to harmonize the intellectualism and theorism of the Stagirite with the diametrically opposed ethics and religion of the Hebrew Bible. And he is apparently unaware of the yawning gulf extending between them. The ethics of the Bible is nothing if not practical. No stress is laid upon knowledge and theoretical speculation as such. . . . That the pentateuchal law is solely concerned with practical conduct—religious, ceremonial, and moral—needs no saying. It is so absolutely clear and evident that one wonders how so clear-sighted a thinker like Maimonides could have been misled by the authority of Aristotle and the intellectual atmosphere of the day to imagine otherwise. (*History of Medieval Jewish Philosophy,* p. 300)

In an early article on Maimonides, Harry Wolfson also emphasized the incompatibility between Maimonides' commitments to philosophy and Jewish law.

> Maimonides was not a rabbi employing Greek logic and categories of thought in order to interpret Jewish religion; he was rather a true medieval Aristotelian using Jewish religion as an illustration of the Stagirite's metaphysical supremacy. Maimonides adheres staunchly to the Law, of course, but his adherence is not the logical consequence of his system. It has its basis in his heredity and practical interests; it is not the logical implication of his philosophy. Judaism designated the established social order of life, in which Maimonides lived and moved and had his being; and it was logically as remote from his intellectual interests as he was historically remote from Aristotle. That, naturally, he was unaware of the dualism must be clear. Indeed he thought he

had made a synthesis and had given scientific demonstrations of poetic conceptions. Therein he was like the Italian priest and astronomer, Pietro Angelo Secchi, who, while performing his religious services, dropped Copernican astronomy, and while in the observatory, dropped his church doctrines. Maimonides really saw no incompatibility between his Judaism and his philosophy; he was a Jew in letter and a philosopher in spirit throughout his life. ("Maimonides and Halevi," pp. 314-15)

Gershom Scholem also believed that Maimonides' philosophy of Judaism was, at bottom, a distortion of rabbinic Judaism while mysticism and Halevi's *Kuzari* were genuinely "Jewish" (*Major Trends in Jewish Mysticism,* pp. 28-29). Both the mystics and Halevi provided models which explained the urgency of revelation and the intrinsic significance of the elaborate ritual structure of Halakhah, whereas Maimonides vainly tried to integrate a few chapters of Aristotelian philosophy into the *Mishneh Torah,* arrogantly ignoring their irrelevance to the legal spirituality of Judaism. In this chapter I shall argue that Maimonides believed that the God of Abraham, Isaac, and Jacob was fundamentally the God of the Philosophers and that in order to be a loyal and committed Jew one must appropriate that God within the "four cubits of Halakhah" (T.B. Berakhot 8a; see my *Maimonides,* pp. 39-65).

One of the primary sections of the *Guide of the Perplexed* is devoted to a subject which Maimonides regarded with the utmost seriousness and which was considered controversial (and still is) in Orthodox religious circles, that is, *ta'amei ha-mitzvot,* providing reasons for the commandments. His bold undertaking on behalf of this thesis placed him at odds with an outspoken group of people whose basic religious sensibilities were thus being challenged. "There is a group of human beings who consider it a grievous thing that causes should be given for any law; what would please them most is that the intellect could not find a meaning for the commandments and prohibitions" (*Guide* 3:31).

Maimonides rejects the classical distinction between *huqqim* and *mishpatim,* which defined the latter as mitzvoth whose social or ethical purposes were evident, and the former, huqqim, as laws and rituals that defy rational explanation. A popular format of many midrashim which deal with polemical issues between Jews and the "nations of the world" relates how those nations and Satan (Israel's perennial accuser) mock Israel because of the huqqim that indicate the irrationality of the Torah and of Israel's claim to revelation.

> Our Rabbis taught: "My ordinances (*mishpatai*) shall you do" (Lev 18:4), that is, such commandments which, if they were not written [in Scripture], they should by right have been written and these are they: [the laws concerning] idolatry [star worship], immorality and bloodshed, robbery and blasphemy. "And My statutes (*huqqotai*) shall you keep" (ibid.), that is, such commandments to which Satan objects, they are [those relating to] the putting on of *sha'atnez* [a garment woven of wool and linen, Deut. 22:11], the *halizah* (Deut. 25:5ff) [performed by] a sister-in-law, the purification of the leper, and the he-goat-to-be-sent-away. And perhaps you might think these are vain things, therefore Scripture says: "I am the Lord" (ibid.), that is, I, the Lord[,] have made it a statute and you have no right to criticize it. (T.B. Yoma 67b)

This use of *huqqim* presupposes the classical distinction.

In the *Guide* 3:25–51, however, Maimonides explains the entire corpus of biblical legislation in terms of three general purposes: eliminating injustice, building moral character, and teaching correct opinions. Maimonides redefined the traditional dichotomy by challenging the notion of reason-less law as an absurdity and arguing that the incomprehensibility of huqqim was the result of human ignorance, not divine intention. Rather than referring to mitzvoth which lack rational or utilitarian reasons, huqqim should be defined as laws whose reasons were once evident but are so no longer. Their irrationality is not part of their inherent nature but is the contingent consequence of historical change. Were we to regain correct knowledge of the historical background of biblical legislation, the mystery of the huqqim would disappear. Maimonides thus overturned the traditional distinction between mishpatim and huqqim by arguing that human ignorance of history and of the sociocultural context of biblical legislation were responsible for the absurd notion of irrational divine legislation.

Maimonides was fully aware of the existence of rabbinic views diametrically opposed to his that advocated silencing those who offered reasons for the commandments (see T.B. Berakhot 33b). He realized that his approach to Halakhah would prove threatening to pious Jews who believed that rationally explaining biblical legislation undermines its religious significance. Nonetheless, he rejected the legitimacy of this response, which he diagnosed as a form of a spiritual pathology.

> What compels them to feel thus is a sickness that they find in their souls, a sickness to which they are unable to give utterance and of which they cannot furnish a satisfactory account. For they think that if those laws were useful in this existence, and had been given to us for this or that reason, it would be as if they derive from the

direction and understanding of some intelligent being. If, however, there is a thing for which the intellect could not find any meaning at all and that does not lead to something useful, it indubitably derives from God; for the reflection of man would not lead to such a thing. It is as if, according to these people of weak intellects, man were more perfect than his Maker; for man speaks and acts in a manner that leads to some intended end, whereas the deity does not act thus, but commands us to do things that are not useful to us and forbids us to do things that are not harmful to us. But He is far exalted above this; the contrary is the case—the whole purpose consisting in what is useful for us, as we have explained on the basis of its dictum: *For our good always, that He might preserve us alive, as it is at this day* (Deut. 6:24). And it says: *Which shall hear all these statutes [huqqim] and say: Surely this great community is a wise and understanding people* (Deut. 4:6). Thus it states explicitly that even all the *statutes [huqqim]* will show to all the nations that they have been given with *wisdom and understanding.* Now if there is a thing for which no reason is known and that does not either procure something useful or ward off something harmful, why should one say of one who believes in it or practices it that he is *wise and understanding* and of great worth? And why should the religious communities think it a wonder? (*Guide* 3:31)

Maimonides' characterization of this religious attitude ignores its possible deeper significance. The people whom Maimonides attacked as spiritually sick deserve a sympathetic hearing. It is not that they believe that God gives irrational laws but that God's laws, as Halevi claimed, cannot be comprehended in terms of what human beings would consider rational and useful. God's ways are not human ways. The category of the religious must be sui generis. Any translation into ordinary cultural, social, or political categories would vitiate its special status and undermine its unique religious significance.

Despite the plausibility of an alternative, more charitable understanding of the antirationalist argument, Maimonides was uncompromising in his rejection and condemnation of it. The biblical text that he repeatedly cited as the clear and unequivocal justification for his position was "See, I have imparted to you laws and rules, as the Lord my God commanded me, for you to abide by in the land which you are about to invade and occupy. Observe them faithfully, for that will be proof of your wisdom and discernment to other peoples, who on hearing of all these laws will say, 'Surely, that great nation is a wise and discerning people'" (Deut. 4:5–6). The fact that the nations of the world would appreciate the laws of the Torah because of their manifest *wisdom and discernment* implied that Israel and the nations of the world shared a common rational universe of discourse that explained their appreciation of the laws of the Torah. This biblical text is the cornerstone of Maimonides' philosophy of Judaism, which is founded on the idea that election and revelation must not remove Israel from participating in a universal rational discourse.

For Maimonides, divine revelation and election do not create, as they do for Halevi, a system of law and beliefs predicated on the uniqueness of the Jewish people. As the eminent Maimonidean scholar Shlomo Pines pointed out, one of the important presuppositions of Maimonides' thought was that Israel's history could be explained by the general laws of history. For Maimonides, election was not incompatible with universality and intelligibility; on the contrary, it was the source of a cultural imperative to translate particularity into universally intelligible terms.

The biblical figure of Adam has often been adopted and

reworked by the fertile imaginations of biblical faiths that transformed him into the prototype of their particular religious ideology. Halevi was not alone in using Adam as the basis of his strong ontological claim in support of the uniqueness and superiority of Judaism and the Jewish people. For Maimonides, the image of God, *zelem 'Elohim,* is not the special, supernatural power God gave to Adam but the faculty of reason, the property by virtue of which human beings differ from all other animals (see *Guide* 1:1). The divine element in human nature is thus natural and universal. Zelem 'Elohim is the essence of both the humanity and the divine element within Jews and non-Jews alike.

In the *Eight Chapters,* Maimonides devotes three chapters to the basic concepts and doctrines of Aristotelian psychology before describing how the mitzvoth develop and restore the health of the human soul. The central theme of this work of ethics is that the principle of the equilibrium, the mean, is the central principle of health not only in the fields of human biology and medicine but equally with respect to the mitzvoth. The mitzvoth aim at cultivating moderation and the virtues of the healthy person as understood by Aristotle in the *Nicomachean Ethics.* Knowledge of Aristotelian psychology is a requirement for understanding the mitzvoth and for understanding the meaning of the Psalmist's words: "the Law of the Lord is perfect restoring the soul" (Ps. 19:9) (*Eight Chapters,* chap. 4).

By showing how the mitzvoth revealed at Sinai are internally related to the ideal of moral health, Maimonides draws attention to the correspondence between the content of revelation and the basic principles of human psychology. This approach conflicts with the religious instincts of many who prefer to view radical singularity as the essential property of the mitzvoth and take pride in proclaiming that the only reason to obey the commandments is because they are commanded.

Another example of the motif of continuity that, like zelem 'Elohim, offers a naturalistic reading of a theological metaphor is *imitatio Dei*. In *Hilkhot De'ot* (Laws concerning character traits), Maimonides notes that the attributes of action attributed to God in the Bible are similar in many ways to the practical virtues according to Aristotelian ethics.

> The right way is the mean in each group of dispositions common to humanity; namely, that disposition which is equally distant from the two extremes in its class, not being nearer to the one than to the other. . . . We are bidden to walk in the middle paths which are the right and proper ways, as it is said, "and thou shalt walk in His ways" (Deut. 28:9). In explanation of the text just quoted, the sages taught, "Even as God is called gracious, so be thou gracious; Even as He is called merciful, so be thou merciful; even as He is called holy, so be thou holy." Thus too the prophets described the Almighty by all the various attributes[,] "long-suffering and abounding in kindness, righteous and upright, perfect, mighty and powerful," and so forth, to teach us, that these qualities are good and right and that a human being should cultivate them, and thus imitate God, as far as he can. . . . And as the Creator is called by these attributes, which constitute the middle path in which we are to walk, this path is called the Way of God and this is what the patriarch Abraham taught his children. ("Laws Concerning Character Traits" 1:4–7)

Maimonides understands the verse "For I have singled him out, that he may instruct his children and his posterity to keep the way of the Lord by doing what is just and right, in order that the Lord may bring about for Abraham what

He has promised" (Gen. 18:19) to mean that Abraham does not require a special revelation to know how to instruct his children "to keep the way of the Lord." All he needs is to understand how virtues are acquired by following the middle path.

The importance of this ethical framework as a source of normative conduct independent of revelation is discussed in several places in the *Guide* (see, for example, 1:54; 3:12, 3:53, 3:54). One instance is Maimonides' "midrash" on Moses' question to God: "Show me Your ways, that I may know You" (Exod. 33:13). The implicit question which sets the stage for Maimonides' interpretation of Moses' request is: What type of knowledge did Moses wish to obtain in addition to what was revealed at Sinai? According to Maimonides, Moses sought knowledge of the divine governance inherent in nature in order to model his political leadership after these natural paradigms. Show me Your ways in nature and I shall imitate Your ways in governing Israel. Israel's way of life must be continuous with God's actions in nature (see *Guide* 1:54).

Maimonides often drew attention to how the natural world mirrored the moral attributes of God. The attribute of justice is revealed in the relative equality of people at birth. Existence is an expression of God's graciousness (*hanun*): "For He, may He be exalted, brings into existence and governs beings that have no claim upon Him with respect to being brought into existence and being governed. For this reason He is called 'gracious.'" (*Guide* 1:54; see also 3:12). *Rahamim* (mercy) can be discerned in the development of the embryo and the wondrous processes of birth and nurturing. Maimonides was appalled by the vulgarity of those who believed they were glorifying God by offering elaborate supernatural descriptions of human conception and birth. The language of miracles makes a travesty of such sublime natural phenomena (see *Guide* 2:6).

Since natural phenomena can have moral significance, then nature as well as history and revelation can serve as a source of ethical values and attitudes. The structure of nature, therefore, is itself a form of divine legislation, and imitatio Dei is its most appropriate human response. Maimonides interpreted the expression "the way of the Lord" with reference to the virtues based on the Aristotelian mean. At the end of the *Guide* (3:54), the halakhic Jew who has acquired knowledge and love of God based on knowledge of God's manifestation in nature discovers a new basis of practice—the imitation of God—which orients him in his return to community.

One of the primary tasks of Maimonides' philosophy of Judaism was to tell the story of revelation, that is, to explain the rationale and purpose of Sinai. For Maimonides, the concept of history is necessary for explaining not only the fact of revelation but also its content and purpose. Unlike the concepts of God and monotheism, revelation has a "story" behind it. As the biblical story of the prehistoric Garden of Eden implies, monotheism existed at the very beginning of history, a figurative way of saying that the idea of monotheism has no essential connection with the idea of history. For Maimonides, Adam and Eve were monotheists naturally. Revelation, on the other hand, has a history that begins with Abraham and culminates with the revelation of the Torah at Sinai.

The interpretation given in the *Mishneh Torah* to the chain of events preceding Sinai in the Laws of Idolatry (chap. 1) is more than a matter of historical interest; it touches on the very meaning and purpose of revelation. Maimonides' original interpretation of the biblical narrative and rabbinic midrash are important sources for understanding his theory of revelation. His distinctive approach stems from his understanding of the relationship between the God of the Philosophers and Judaism.

The concepts of nature and history are so rich in associations and connotations that they often serve as grand metaphors for entire worldviews and sensibilities. This is especially true with respect to the philosophical outlooks of Maimonides and Halevi, in which the main intellectual and spiritual concepts underlying their philosophies of Judaism are closely related to these notions. In the case of Maimonides, the nature-history distinction lies at the root of a comprehensive and consistent theory of Judaism.

In Maimonides' view, nature and being ("creation") refer to a framework in which the individual's primary goal in life is to acquire knowledge of reality through the study of physics and metaphysics in order to contemplate the eternal truths of being and, ultimately, the most perfect being, the first cause, the necessary existent, the *'ehyeh 'asher 'ehyeh*. As a spiritual framework, it is a theocentric metaphysical world which human beings "enter" only through the intellect, whose aim is disinterested love of God. The language of philosophy is universal and culturally independent, and the reality it seeks to know is eternal and fixed. The language of physics and metaphysics, the language of creation, mirrors the timeless unchanging perfection of existence. Its logic is the logic of truth and perfection.

The logic of history, however, is completely different. Its terrain is marked by movement and change, by detours and compromises. Its reality is best conveyed by narrative, where the past informs the present and the present the future. Metaphysical realities have no history; they are timeless and static. Historical realities, however, incorporate their past in their present; to understand what is, one must understand what was.

The language of history is essentially dynamic. What occurs is not the expression of ideal Platonic forms but a "compromise" reached in the ever present negotiations between past, present, and future. Creation ex nihilo is the paradigm of divine action without constraint. Revelation in history, on the other hand, is action within limits and constraints. In contrast to the logic of creation, the logic of history conveys accommodation and compromise.

In the "Laws of Idolatry," Maimonides traces the historical origins of idolatry to a mistake in practice, namely, mistaken forms of worship, which evolved into idolatrous practices and beliefs. Although the original content of religious belief under the influence of natural reason was monotheistic, it became corrupted by a chain of events that began with an intellectual mistake which ultimately led to the proliferation of incorrect forms of worship and the disappearance of belief in God.

> In the days of Enosh, the people fell into gross error, and the counsel of the wise men of the generation became foolish. Enosh himself was among those who erred. Their error was as follows: "Since God," they said, "created these stars and spheres to guide

the world, set them on high and allotted unto them honor, and since they are ministers who minister before Him, they deserve to be praised and glorified, and honor should be rendered them; and it is the will of God, blessed be He, that men should aggrandize and honor those whom He aggrandized and honored—just as a king desires that respect should be shown to the officers who stand before Him, and thus honor is shown to the king." When this idea arose in their minds, they began to erect temples to the stars, offered up sacrifices . . . their purpose, according to their perverse notions, being to obtain the Creator's favor. This was the root of idolatry. . . . All know that Thou alone art God; their error and folly consists in imagining that this vain worship is Thy desire. ("Laws of Idolatry" 1:1)

By the time of Abraham paganism had spread throughout the world, but owing to his great intellectual efforts and the unshakable certitude of his understanding of the natural world, Abraham was able to free himself from the pagan influences of his environment.

The world moved on in this [pagan, idolatrous] fashion, till that Pillar of the World, the Patriarch Abraham, was born. After he was weaned, while still an infant, his mind began to reflect. By day and by night he was thinking and wondering: "How is it possible that this (celestial) sphere should continuously be guiding the world and have no one to guide it and cause it to turn round; for it cannot be that it turns round of itself." He had no teacher, no one to instruct him in aught. He was submerged, in Ur of Chaldees, among silly idolaters. His father and mother and the entire population worshipped idols, and he worshipped with them. But his mind was busily working and reflecting till he had attained the way of truth, apprehended the correct line of thought and knew that there is One God, that He guides the celestial Sphere and created everything, and that among all that exist, there is no god beside Him. . . . Abraham was forty years old when he recognized his Creator. ("Laws of Idolatry" 1:2)

In describing Abraham's spiritual journey from paganism to monotheism, Maimonides goes into unusually great detail on the various stages of the philosophical quest pursued by this cultural and religious iconoclast. Abraham's discovery of God is a paradigm of philosophical spirituality. It is slow and gradual, for unlike the sudden, vertical effect on belief of witnessing God's miracles, philosophical beliefs are the products of a sustained, painstaking process of rational inquiry.

The biographical material presented in the *Guide* (3:29) and the *Mishneh Torah* concerning Abraham's personal spiritual quest and his attempt at building a community of knowers of God is meant to refer to the period in Abraham's life *before* God told him, "Go forth" (Gen. 12:1). In other words, the election of Abraham occurred after his independent discovery of God in nature and his break with the pagan culture of his day. His election was not a radically unexpected act of grace that cast doubt on his previous way of life (as Halevi claimed) but a confirmation of what he had already discovered about God in nature through independent reason and reflection.

To best appreciate the religious implications of this position, we should consider the perennial popularity of arguments for establishing certainty about God's existence similar to those presented in the *Kuzari*. Halevi was convinced that belief in the divine reality must be based on a direct, unmediated experience of God. The quintessential basis for establishing belief in God's existence was the occurrence of miracle.

It is no wonder that those who opposed Maimonides and claimed that the concepts of election and revelation implied that Abraham rose above the deficiencies of philosophical religion presented a very different biographical portrait of Abraham's discovery of God. The antiphilosophical emphasis of the vertical dimension of revelation is graphically driven home by the midrashic statement that Abraham came to know God as a three-year-old. The Rabad, in his glosses to the *Mishneh Torah,* takes Maimonides to task for selecting the alternative opinion, which claims that Abraham was forty. This seemingly trivial disagreement is in fact a clash of two very different religious sensibilities. Whereas forty is an appropriate age for philosophical wisdom, three forces us to introduce the notion of divine grace. If, as the Rabad claims, Abraham was three years old, then philosophical reflection had nothing to do with his election.

After making his great discovery, Abraham turned outward toward the community and began teaching others about the truth of monotheism, persuading them to abandon their idolatrous ways. Unlike the prototype of philosophical religion described by Halevi, who is passionless and lacks the courage to die for his beliefs, Maimonides' Abraham is a man who, not content with his personal intellectual achievement, must share his new understanding with others, regardless of risk.

> Having attained this knowledge, he began to refute the inhabitants of Ur of the Chaldees, arguing with them. . . . When he had prevailed over them with his arguments, the king (of the country) sought to slay him. He was miraculously saved, and emigrated to Haran. He then began to proclaim to the whole world with great power and to instruct the people that the entire Universe had but one Creator and that Him it was right to worship. He went from city to city and from kingdom to kingdom, calling and

gathering together the inhabitants till he arrived in the land of Canaan. There too, he proclaimed his message, as it is said "And he called there on the name of the Lord, God of the Universe" (Gen. 21:33). When the people flocked to him and questioned him regarding his assertions, he would instruct each one according to his capacity till he had brought him to the way of truth, and thus thousands and tens of thousands joined him. These were the persons referred to in the phrase, "men of the house of Abraham." He implanted in their hearts this great doctrine, composed books on it, and taught it to Isaac, his son. ("Laws of Idolatry" 1:2)

Abraham's discovery of God in nature engenders a love for God and a religious enthusiasm that moved him not only to build a community but to be prepared to face martyrdom. We should bear in mind that the community Abraham establishes is a philosophical creation, that is, a community based on a shared intellectual understanding of God achieved through the persuasive power of rational argument. The verb Maimonides used most frequently to describe Abraham, Isaac, and Jacob's activities was *lelamed,* "to teach." Abraham does not command or legislate; he argues and demonstrates. In contrast to Moses, the Patriarchs do not speak in the language of legislative authority. Nevertheless, they establish a community of knowers of God (*'umma she-hi yoda'at 'et ha-shem*).

The "nation of knowers of God" was not able to withstand the corrupting forces of Egyptian paganism. Revelation and the necessity for divine legislation emerge in the wake of this failure. According to Maimonides, pre-Sinaitic history set the stage for Mosaic revelation by indicating the vulnerability of human society to the corrupting influences of paganism and the insufficiency of the philosophical ideal as the exclusive organizing principle of a community of believers.

> The patriarch Jacob instructed all his sons, set apart Levi, appointed him head (teacher) and placed him in a college to teach the way of God and keep the charge of Abraham. He charged his sons to appoint from the tribe of Levi, one instructor after another, in uninterrupted succession, so that the doctrine might never be forgotten. And so it went on with ever increasing vigor among Jacob's children and their adherents till they became a people that knew God. When the Israelites had stayed a long while in Egypt, they relapsed, learnt the practices of their neighbors, and, like them, worshipped idols, with the exception of the tribe of Levi, which steadfastly kept the charge of the Patriarch. This tribe of Levi never practised idolatry. ("Laws of Idolatry" 1:2)

Moses, therefore, is a political statesman. He is the prophet par excellence. Unlike Abraham, he speaks not only with the persuasive force of rational argumentation but also with the power and authority of divine legislation. With the advent of Moses, a new category emerges: the category of mitzvah. This idea is explicitly articulated in the *Guide* (2:39):

> Not one of the prophets—such as the Patriarchs, Shem, Eber, Noah, Methuselah, and Enoch—who came before Moses our Master, has ever said to a class of people: God has sent me to you and has commanded me to say to you such and such things; He has forbidden you to do such and such things and has commanded you to do such and such things. This is a thing that is not attested to by any text of the Torah and that does not figure in any true tradition. These men only received prophetic revelation from God according to what we have set forth. He who

received a great overflow, as for instance, Abraham, assembled the people and called them by the way of teaching and instruction to adhere to the truth that he had grasped. Thus Abraham taught the people and explained to them by means of speculative proofs that the world has but one deity, that He has created all the things that are other than Himself, and that none of the forms and no created things in general ought to be worshipped. This is what he instructed the people in, attracting them by means of eloquent speeches and by means of the benefits he conferred upon them. But he never said: God has sent me to you and has given me commandments and prohibitions.

As indicated above, pre-Sinaitic history is important for Maimonides because of the idea that revelation is an event with a history. The realities of history called for a new form of communal life, a community of mitzvah, law, and authority. In order that the way of Abraham continue, it was now necessary to incorporate the idea of a community of knowers of God into a national-political framework, because

the doctrine implanted by Abraham would, in a very short time, have been uprooted, and Jacob's descendants would have relapsed into the error and perversities universally prevalent. But because of God's love for us and because He kept the oath made to our ancestor Abraham, He appointed Moses to be our teacher and the teacher of all the prophets, and charged him with his mission. After Moses had begun to exercise his prophetic functions and Israel had been chosen by the Almighty as His heritage, he crowned them with precepts, and showed them the way to worship Him and how to deal with idolatry and with those who go astray after it. ("Laws of Idolatry" 1:2)

This historic insight informs and shapes the key concepts of revelation, the Torah, election, and prophecy. The idea that revelation is not inherently related to the concept of God as the ground of being stands in sharp contrast to many mystical conceptions of the relation between revelation and creation. It appears that according to Maimonides' understanding of the biblical narrative, revelation and the election of Israel were contingent events. Only after experience showed that a "nation that knows God" was unable to withstand the allure of paganism did the need for law and legislative prophecy become evident. The God of revelation is, as it were, conditioned by historical rather than cosmic processes. The "necessity" for revelation is not contained in the moment of creation but, rather, in a moment of human history—a moment that reveals human vulnerability and the need for authority and law.

It is important to note that Maimonides states that the philosophical elite represented by the tribe of Levi were able to withstand the allure of paganism by virtue of their philosophical knowledge of God. Revelation, law, and legislative authority are essential, however, when we are concerned with a whole nation, not simply with a remnant comprised of philosophers.

For Halevi, *qorbanot* (sacrifices) are perfect examples of the nonrational, ahistorical ritualistic meaning of Halakhah. The institution of qorbanot symbolizes the uniqueness of the Torah as the framework of a spiritual way of life beyond what unaided human reason can provide. The sacrificial cult was a clear example of the discontinuity between Mosaic revealed religion and philosophical spirituality. Performing the sacrificial rite in the prescribed manner expressed and nurtured the divine capacity found only in this unique people. For Maimonides, qorbanot pointed to the fact that the Jewish people are subject to the same vulnerabilities as all human beings. The laws dealing with sacrifices are concrete symbols of the constraints history places on all forms of social and religious development and of the biblical principles of compromise and accommodation.

Halevi accepted the all-inclusive framework of Halakhah as his starting point and ultimate frame of reference. The incomprehensible aspects of Judaism could be understood so long as we were prepared to revise our theories of psychology and history accordingly. The details of Halakhah indicated that Israel was not like the other nations; its spiritual needs were unique, and hence its normative way of life differed from that of other nations.

For Halevi one must understand the nature of Jewish religion in order to understand human nature; for Maimonides one must understand human nature in order to understand the Torah. For Halevi one must posit an ontological hierarchy in which the spiritual stands above the rational and the prophet is qualitatively different from the philosopher in order to make the biblical historical narrative and legislation intelligible. For Maimonides the opposite is the case. Only by grasping universal human nature and the structure of the natural order can one appreciate the inherent wisdom of revelation. Maimonides turned to history and psychology to interpret biblical and rabbinic law. If we knew all there was to know about ancient Sabian culture and practices current at the time of revelation, we would understand everything there is to know about the huqqim (see *Guide* 3:49). When we examine the content of revelation, what is most striking is not the uniqueness of Israel but, on the contrary, the common humanity shared by Israel and the rest of the world. The prophecy of Moses arose in response to the seductions of idolatry. Because Israel was similar to all the nations it was vulnerable to pagan influences. The Bible legislated the qorbanot and many other laws in order to gradually wean the community away from idolatry. The biblical promises of rewards and punishments are intelligible only when one realizes that the people of Israel are subject to the hungers, fears, and need for economic security present in all human societies (see *Guide* 3:37).

Maimonides explained the reason for including sacrificial worship in the Bible in terms of his notion of the "divine ruse" that informs God's actions in nature.

> Many things in our Law are due to something similar to this very governance on the part of Him who governs, may He be glorified and exalted. For a sudden transition from one opposite to another is impossible. And therefore man, according to his nature, is not capable of abandoning suddenly all to which he was accustomed. ... And as at that time the way of life generally accepted and customary in the whole world and the universal service upon which we were brought up consisted in offering various species of living beings in the temples in which images were set up, in worshipping the latter, and in burning incense before them—the pious ones and the ascetics being at that time, as we have explained, the people who were devoted to the service of the temples consecrated to the stars—: His wisdom, may He be exalted, and His gracious ruse, which is manifest in regard to all His creatures, did not require that He give us a Law prescribing the rejection, abandonment, and abolition [of] all these kinds of worship. For one could not then conceive the acceptance of [such a Law], considering the nature of man, which always likes that to which it is accustomed. At that time this would have been similar to the appearance of a prophet in these times who, calling upon the people

to worship God, would say: "God has given you a Law forbidding you to pray to Him, to fast, to call upon Him for help in misfortune. Your worship should consist solely in meditation without any works at all." (*Guide* 3:32)

In order to eradicate idolatry (if not immediately, then eventually), the divine legislator used a "ruse"—a legal strategy aimed at modifying behavior through a gradual process of change. The notion of the ruse represents the distinctive way biblical legislation waged war against idolatry, that is, not directly, by legislative fiat, but indirectly, by legislative accommodation. Instead of rejecting pagan forms of worship, God incorporated them into the sanctuary and temple rites. The practice of sacrifices was, however, subjected to numerous restrictions with respect to persons, circumstances, and location in order to diminish its popularity and eventually wean people from this imperfect form of worship.

For one kind of worship—I mean the offering of sacrifices—even though it was done in His name, may He be exalted, was not prescribed to us in the way it existed at first; I mean to say in such a way that sacrifices could be offered in every place and at every time. Nor could a temple be set up in any fortuitous place, nor could any fortuitous man offer the sacrifice: "Whosoever would, he consecrated him" (I King 13:33). On the contrary, he forbade all this and established one single house [as the temple], "Unto the place which the Lord shall chose" (Deut. 12:26), so that sacrifices should not be offered elsewhere: "That thou offer not thy burnt-offerings in every place that thou seest" (Deut. 12:13). Also only the offspring of one particular family can be "Priest(s)." All this was intended to restrict this kind of worship, so that only the portion of it should subsist whose abolition is not required by His wisdom. On the other hand, invocation and prayers are made in every place and by anyone whoever he may be. (*Guide* 3:32)

For Maimonides, God's manifestation of love for Israel was expressed in His acceptance of human weaknesses. The revelation of the Torah mirrors the decision of the divine educator to wait for the people of Israel to gradually give up the forms of behavior to which they were accustomed. In order to help the reader understand why God permitted sacrifices in the biblical period, Maimonides draws an analogy between that time and his own in a provocative manner: "For one could not then conceive the acceptance of [such a Law], considering the nature of man, which always likes that to which it is accustomed. At that time this would have been similar to the appearance of a prophet in these times who, calling upon the people to worship God, would say: 'God has given you a Law forbidding you to pray to Him, to fast, to call upon Him for help in misfortune. Your worship should consist solely in meditation without any works at all'" (*Guide* 3.32).

Maimonides' explanation of the inclusion of sacrifices in biblical law is a classic example of his theory of accommodation. The sacrificial cult is not a high point in the history of religion but a vestigial reminder of Israel's pagan past. Sacrifices fall below petitional prayer and contemplation in Maimonides' hierarchy of forms of worship. What then prompted the divine legislator to include sacrifices in the Torah? If the central goal of the Torah was to have Israel repudiate idolatry and pagan forms of worship, why were sacrifices not excluded from the revealed law so that higher forms of worship could be incorporated immediately?

In response to the question of why God does not change the nature of human beings to act in accordance with His first intention and thus be free of the pagan habits acquired in Egypt, Maimonides answers, "God does not change at all the nature of human individuals by means of miracles. . . . We do not say this because we believe that the changing of the nature of any human individual is difficult for Him. . . . Rather is it possible and fully within capacity. But according to the foundations of the Law, of the Torah, He has never willed to do it, nor shall He ever will it. For if it were His will that the nature of any human individual should be changed because of what He, may He be exalted, wills from that individual, sending of prophets and all giving of a Law would have been useless" (*Guide* 3:32).

Since God doesn't change human nature, the law must take account of the nature of the people it addresses. In a word, the principle of divine behavior in human history and especially in revelation is accommodation. The meaning of the Torah reflects God's acting in history not through the power of miracle but as an educator.

The same principle of accommodation informs God's decision to take the roundabout rather than the direct and shorter route to the Promised Land (Exod. 13:17–18; *Guide* 3:32). Whereas a literal reading of the biblical story would suggest that the forty-year sojourn in the desert was a punishment for disobedience (see Num. 14), Maimonides explained that in order for the people of Israel to fight against the Canaanites, they had to shed the slave mentality they had acquired during years of Egyptian servitude.

> For just as it is not in the nature of man that, after having been brought up in slavish service occupied with clay, bricks, and similar things, he should all of a sudden wash off from his hands the dirt deriving from them and proceed immediately to fight against *the children of 'Anaq,* so is it also not in his nature that, after having

been brought up upon very many modes of worship and of customary practices, which the souls find so agreeable that they become as it were a primary notion, he should abandon them all of a sudden. And just as the deity used a gracious ruse in causing them to wander perplexedly in the desert until their souls became courageous—it being well known that life in the desert and lack of comforts for the body necessarily develop courage whereas the opposite circumstances necessarily develop cowardice—and until, moreover, people were born who were not accustomed to humiliation and servitude . . . so did this group of laws derive from a divine grace, so that they should be left with the kind of practices to which they were accustomed and so that consequently the belief, which constitutes the first intention, should be validated in them. (*Guide* 3:32)

The forty-year sojourn in the desert thus expressed God's patience and acceptance of the slow process of human change, from a people suffering feelings of impotence and inferiority to a confident people able to assume responsibility for their destiny. God, the lawgiver and lord of history, acts in response to the human condition. Revelation is divine speech informed by the human reality.

The permanence of Mosaic law can be explained in terms of Maimonides' faith in the continuity of history as we know it. Maimonides believed that the Torah is the most perfect instrument for dealing with the problematic conditions of human existence (see *Guide* 2:40). And barring a radical transformation of history and human nature (which Maimonides was prepared to rule out "metaphysically" by accepting the doctrine of eternity *a parte post,* from that moment), the most one can hope for in history is messianism, an amelioration rather than a radical transformation of history. In other words, the law of Moses is permanent because the problematic conditions for which it is the best possible solution are permanent. One can argue that Maimonides' claim regarding the permanence of Mosaic law implied that he believed that messianic times, like all historical phenomena, were contingent and temporary, no matter how long-lasting.

Although history is important to both Maimonides and Halevi, their understandings of biblical descriptions of God's actions in history differ significantly. Given Maimonides' theory of accommodation and his model of God as educator, biblical descriptions of divine actions in history need not be understood as miraculous ruptures in the natural order. For Halevi, however, the God of Abraham, Isaac, and Jacob—the God revealed in the liberation drama of Exodus—can be understood only by positing a radical discontinuity between the orderly patterns of nature and God's providential actions in history.

According to Maimonides, Moses was Abraham's true spiritual successor in the war against idolatry. Their ultimate beliefs and aims were the same, even though their weapons and tactics (philosophy and rational persuasion versus sacrifice and revealed legislation) differed. Despite the contrast between Abraham the teacher and Moses the legislator, Maimonides treats them in terms of their essential continuity. Moses follows Abraham not only temporally but also spiritually. Symbolically, this continuity is conveyed by the practice of circumcision, which is a constant sign that the covenant between God and Abraham is both the founding idea and ultimate telos of Mosaic law.

In the *Guide* (3:49) Maimonides offers two reasons for circumcision: to diminish sexual passion and to draw attention to the Abrahamic covenant and thus instill a sense of solidarity among people who share a common belief in the unity of God. Circumcision is not a sign of surrender to a normative system that defies comprehension. It is a symbol that unites the Jewish people through the common language of the Abrahamic covenant. In the *Mishneh Torah,* Maimonides adds a third reason: to serve as a sign upon our flesh that we must love God at all times (hence the laws of circumcision were included in "The Book of Love" in the *Mishneh Torah*).

Maimonides' account of Abraham's philosophical spirituality may prove threatening in that the ultimate ideal of this outlook does not depend exclusively on Halakhah. Why should Jews expose themselves to persecution and suffering on account of their commitment to Torah and Halakhah if knowledge and love of God are attainable by following the path of a philosophical spirituality? We can therefore understand the popular rabbinic tradition that also assumes the continuity of Abraham and Moses in a reverse direction: that is, it superimposes the legal framework of Judaism on the biblical character of Abraham. According to this classical form of traditionalist thinking, Abraham is a prototype of halakhic Judaism. If the biblical story indicates the contrary (for example, Abraham's violation of basic rabbinic rules of *kashrut* [dietary laws]; see Genesis 18), then the midrashic commentator must touch up the embarrassing details. In the end Abraham fulfills all the laws of the Torah (including the laws of Passover, well in advance of the exodus from Egypt!). Instead of viewing Abraham as a philosopher the rabbis portray him as a meticulously observant halakhic Jew (see T.B. Yoma 28b).

In spite of the legitimacy of such fears, Maimonides did not conceal his belief in the possibility of singular individuals achieving spiritual excellence through intellectual love of God independent of the community of Israel and the framework of Halakhah. If we recall Maimonides' claim that the tribe of Levi—the remnant of Abraham's community of knowers of God—withstood the allure of paganism as a result of their philosophical knowledge of God we can appreciate Maimonides' inclusion of the universal ideal of the Abrahamic philosophical love of God in his treatment of the sanctity of the tribe of Levi.

> Why was the Tribe of Levi granted no right to a share in the Land of Israel and in its spoils, together with his brothers? Because they were set apart to worship the Lord, to serve Him, and to teach His upright ways and His righteous judgments to the many, as it is said, "They shall teach Jacob Thine ordinances, and Israel Thy law" (Deut. 33:10). They were consequently set apart from the ways of the world: they may not wage war as do the rest of Israel, they have no share in the Land, and they may acquire nothing for themselves by physical force. They are rather the host of the Holy Name, as it is said, "Bless, Lord, his host" (Deut. 33:11). It is He, blessed be He, who acquires [goods] for them, as it is said, "I am thy portion and thine inheritance" (Num. 18:20).
>
> Not only the Tribe of Levi, but also each and every individual of those who come into the world, whose spirit moves him and whose knowledge gives him understanding to set himself apart in order to stand before the Lord, to serve Him, to worship Him, and to know Him, who walks upright as God had made him to do, and releases his neck from the yoke of the many speculations that the children of man are wont to pursue—such an individual is consecrated to the Holy of Holies, and his portion and inheritance shall be in the Lord forever and ever more. The Lord will grant him in this world whatsoever is sufficient for him, the same as He had granted to the priests and to the Levites. Thus indeed

did David, upon whom be peace, say, "Lord, the portion of mine inheritance and of my cup, Thou maintainest my lot" (Ps. 16:5). ("Laws of Sabbatical and Jubilee Years" 13:12–13)

Simply stated, neither ethnicity nor biology is an essential condition for becoming *nahalat ha-shem*, God's "portion and inheritance." All who walk in the spiritual ways of Abraham share the same holiness as the tribe of Levi. *Qedusha* (holiness) is not a genetic property unique to the people of Israel. Although the service of God was institutionalized and holiness turned into a property legally defined by biology, geography, and nationality, a deeper understanding of qedusha posits a universal ideal transcending racial and national distinctions and ritual forms of worship. Halakhah and revelation notwithstanding, the fact is that "each and every individual . . . whose spirit moves him and whose knowledge gives him understanding . . . to stand before the Lord, to serve Him . . . such an individual is consecrated to the Holy of Holies, and his portion and inheritance shall be in the Lord forever and ever more."

According to Maimonides' typological analysis of biblical history, Abraham is important in showing that the Jewish tradition acknowledged the legitimacy of a spiritual way independent of Torah and mitzvah. The most radical implication of the story of Abraham is that the founding principle of Judaism is not halakhic. In contrast to Halevi, for whom the God of Abraham, Isaac, and Jacob is accessible only to those who possess the unique, ontological spiritual power implanted by God at the moment of creation, Maimonides makes this God available to all who embrace him regardless of biological origin. This distinction is also significant for understanding the different approaches of Maimonides and Halevi to the status of the convert (compare Maimonides' "Letter to Obadiah the Proselyte" with Halevi's *Kuzari* 1:27, 115).

In contrast to the rabbinic dictum "God in His world has only the four cubits of Halakhah," Maimonides places the universal philosophical ideal, attainable by Jew and non-Jew alike, within the four cubits (see Maimonides' introduction to the Commentary to the *Mishneh*). The fact that the *Mishneh Torah* begins with several chapters on physics, metaphysics, and philosophy and ends with the theme of messianism expresses the centrality of the philosophical religious ideal in his code of law.

> The Sages and Prophets did not long for the days of the Messiah that Israel might exercise dominion over the world, or rule over the heathens, or be exalted by the nations, or that it might eat and drink and rejoice. Their aspiration was that Israel be free to devote itself to the Law and its wisdom, with no one to oppress or disturb it, and thus be worthy of life in the world to come. In that era there will be neither famine nor war, neither jealousy nor strife. Blessings will be abundant, comforts within the reach of all. The one preoccupation of the whole world will be to know the Lord. Hence Israelites will be very wise, they will know the things that are now concealed and will attain an understanding of their Creator to the utmost capacity of the human mind, as it is written: "For the earth shall be full of the knowledge of the Lord, as the waters cover the sea" (Is. 11:9). ("Kings and Wars" 12:4–5)

For gifted individuals who can realize the ideal of intellectual love of God independent of political and socioeconomic conditions, Maimonides offers his *Guide of the Perplexed.* For the broader community, however, the goal of Judaism can be achieved only if the conditions of history change and people become free to pursue the love and knowledge of God. One's conception of God and the life of worship are conditioned by the cultural and material conditions of history. This is the essence of Maimonides' messianism, which is treated elaborately in his commentary to *Helek* and in the *Mishneh Torah* but ignored in the *Guide of the Perplexed.*

The interaction between intellectual love of God and the anthropocentric world that revolves around mitzvah and Halakhah are conveyed in the *Mishneh Torah* by the two eschatological doctrines of 'olam ha-ba (the world to come; immortality) and messianism. Messianism anchors Judaism within community and history; 'olam ha-ba energizes the individual by the pathos of disinterested love of God independent of Judaism's triumph and vindication in history. Maimonides ends the Book of Knowledge of the *Mishneh Torah* ("Laws of Repentance" 8–9) with a description of the system of Halakhah that is rooted in history but nevertheless points to a transhistorical ideal ('olam ha-ba).

The driving force behind Judaism is to overcome paganism, and to this end Judaism uses utilitarian, anthropocentric principles to formulate laws and beliefs for building the best community possible. Ultimately, however, the system has meaning only to the degree that it creates the conditions for transcending itself, that is, for transcending history and history-bound consciousness by following the path of philosophy to the knowledge and love of God.

Halevi and Maimonides are often compared in terms of the basic question "Whose philosophy of Judaism mirrors the authentic Jewish worldview?" Gershom Scholem, Samson Raphael Hirsch, and others have claimed that of the two,

Halevi is the true Jewish philosopher because he articulated a philosophy of Judaism in which mitzvah, Halakhah, and history are pivotal concepts.

Maimonides, however, has always been problematic. It is no wonder that his writings have been a source of dismay to scholars and traditionalists alike. To compare the sanctity of anyone devoted to an intellectual love of God to the sanctity of the tribe of Levi, to interpret the Song of Songs—traditionally understood to describe the intimate love between God and Israel—as a description of the intellectual love of any human being for God, to claim that halakhists, however pious, who lack philosophical knowledge cannot enter the inner chambers of the palace of the King (*Guide* 3:51), to ignore messianism and the yearning for historical redemption and to make the disembodied intellectual love of God ('olam ha-ba) the ultimate telos of Judaism—all these are perplexing in the light of the significance given to praxis (halakhic observance) and to the unique status of Jews as God's elect in the tradition.

The biblical scholar Nehama Leibowitz once asked me about the plausibility of Maimonides' interpretation of God's self-naming in Exodus 3:14: *'ehyeh 'asher 'ehyeh*. Maimonides understands this as "I am that I am," which he explains as "the existent that is the existent or the necessarily existent" (*Guide* 1:63). Leibowitz questioned whether this would answer the concerns of Jewish slaves in Egypt. Did Maimonides believe that the first question they posed to Moses would be philosophical? Is God's necessary rather than contingent existence the most appropriate theological statement to make to slaves awaiting liberation?

Yehuda Halevi understands *'ehyeh* as: "I will be with

you. I will be present when you seek Me." The important message for Halevi is that despite the uncertainty of freedom, we must know that God will not abandon us. Are Maimonides' critics not justified in claiming that Halevi's event-based theology better reflects the essence of Judaism? Aren't one's credentials as a traditional Jewish thinker undermined when one substitutes the impersonal God of the Philosophers for the God of the Bible?

In the next chapter I shall analyze themes in the talmudic tradition that I believe enabled Maimonides to appropriate the God of the Philosophers. I shall argue that only by moving away from dependence on events as manifestations of God's love can a person withstand the temptations of idolatry. If one's whole sense of the life of faith depends upon a miracle-based conception of providence and the biblical promises of reward and punishment, then one risks exchanging God for alternative sources of well-being and security. The fundamental issue in the battle against idolatry is to prevent this from happening. Maimonides believed that philosophical religion was necessary in order to overcome idolatry. Only a theological understanding of God as the necessary being could provide a metahistorical frame of reference. The talmudic tradition kept alive the idea of a personal God by shifting the emphasis from an event-based to a text-centered culture.

It is no accident that some of the major topics of the *Kuzari* are absent from the *Guide,* for example, the meaning of Jewish exile, a theology of history, and a polemical confrontation with Christianity and Islam. In the whole of the *Guide,* Maimonides never once introduces the idea of a redemptive scheme for history nor does he connect the vitality of Judaism with a historical transformation of the Jewish people. His overriding concern is for the problematic situation and integrity of the individual Jew. Whereas the *Kuzari* is concerned with the historical need to revitalize the Jewish people, the *Guide* openly expresses its preference for the single individual over "a thousand ignoramuses." Here the vitality of Judaism is measured not by its ability to become a redemptive force in history but by its ability to retain the committed, observant Jew who is a student of philosophy within the framework of Halakhah (see the introduction to the *Guide*).

Maimonides believed that the only way to do this was to support and encourage those students of the Torah and philosophy who felt confused or filled with religious doubt. Halevi was critical of philosophy for *causing* confusion and uncertainty; Maimonides was not afraid of creating religious perplexity. In fact, I would argue that he believed that we can move from a naive to a mature love of God and the Torah only through struggle with religious uncertainty and confusion.

Careful reading of the *Guide* often leads to that confusion rather than to certainty. Shlomo Pines once remarked to me that there are at least four different plausible interpretations of the *Guide*. It is a book filled with contradictions and radical suggestions which force the student to carefully ponder its subtle and suggestive depths. A serious reading of the *Guide* will leave one wondering what Maimonides' beliefs were about the creation and the eternity of the universe, individual and general providence, and the relation between thought and practice and between petitional and contemplative prayer, along with many other issues. Although Maimonides can appear to be a dogmatic religious rationalist who formulated the thirteen principles of faith and claimed that Jews who did not accept them should be excluded from the community of Israel, those who read the *Guide* without presuppositions will discover that those "dogmatic" principles are in fact quite ambiguous. Maimonides devoted his life to educating Jews and convincing them to love and be loyal to their tradition. But he did not believe that loyalty required insulation from Islamic and Greek philosophy or that Torah and Halakhah were the only ways for an individual to worship and love God.

# CHAPTER FOUR

# Rabbinic Foundations of Maimonides' Thought

In his role as leader and educator of the Jewish community, Moses Maimonides follows the path of the biblical Moses in his relentless, uncompromising battle against idolatry (see *Guide* 1:36). Whereas for Yehuda Halevi the significance of the election of Israel is the revelation of God through the events of Israel's history, for Maimonides election means that Israel is called upon to struggle against idolatry. The *Mishneh Torah* and the *Guide of the Perplexed* are obsessed with the theme of idolatry. The introductory chapters of the *Mishneh Torah*, which Gershom Scholem considered completely unrelated to a life of Halakhah, were for Maimonides the soul of halakhic Judaism and its ultimate telos. In the light of the rabbinic tradition Maimonides wrote: "One who acknowledges idolatry rejects the entire Torah and one who rejects idolatry acknowledges the entire Torah. And this is the fundamental principle of all the commandments" ("Laws of Idolatry" 2:4; see *Guide* 3:29).

In "The Laws of Repentance," Maimonides offers the following definition of the heretic: "Five classes are termed Heretics; he who says that there is no God and the world has no ruler; he who says that there is a ruling power but that it is vested in two or more persons; he who says that there is one ruler, but that He is a body and has form; he who denies that He alone is the First Cause and Rock of the Universe; likewise, he who renders worship to anyone besides Him, to serve as a mediator between the human being and the Lord of the Universe. Whoever belongs to any of these five classes is termed a heretic" (3:7). Maimonides considers a belief that God has a body and form similar to a belief that there is no God or a belief in polytheism. This evoked the rage of the Rabad: "Why has he called such a person a heretic? There are many people greater than and superior to him who adhere to such a belief on the basis of what they have seen in verses of Scripture and even more in the words of those *aggadot* which can cause confusion regarding philosophical ideas."

The Rabad could not agree with the idea that a Jew who lived by the Halakhah was a heretic. How could a person who obeyed the law, followed the commandments, and was committed to every detail of the discipline of Halakhah but who believed in the corporeality of God because of a literal reading of the Bible and rabbinic haggadoth be classified as a heretic?

Maimonides was undoubtedly aware of the likelihood of such objections, yet his opposition to false notions of God was uncompromising.

If, however, it should occur to you that one who believes in the corporeality of God should be excused because of his having been brought up in this doctrine or because of his ignorance and the shortcomings of his apprehension, you ought to hold a similar belief with regard to *an idolater;* for he only worships idols because of his ignorance or because of his upbringing: *They continue in the custom of their fathers.* If, however, you should say that the external sense of the biblical text causes men to fall into this doubt, you ought to know that *an idolater* is similarly impelled to his idolatry by imaginings and defective representations. Accordingly there is no excuse for one who does not accept the authority of men who inquire into the truth and are engaged in speculation if he himself is incapable of engaging in such speculation. I do not consider as an infidel one who cannot demonstrate that the corporeality of God should be negated. But I do consider as an infidel one who does not believe in its negation; and this particularly in view of the existence of the interpretations of *Onqelos* and of *Yonathan ben Uziel,* may peace be on both of them, who cause their readers to keep away as far as possible from the belief in the corporeality of God. (*Guide* 1:36)

Maimonides did not accept the tradition that condemned idolatry outside the Jewish community but tolerated it within. He argued that if one excused Jews for mistakenly believing in God's corporeality because of a literal misreading of the Bible, then one ought to hold a similarly charitable view toward gentile idolaters who worshiped idols from ignorance or because of their cultural upbringing.

Maimonides regarded the demand to reject idolatry as the central concern of Halakhah. Toleration of anything that might lead, in any way whatsoever, to idolatry is categorically forbidden by the law. Maimonides codified the halakhah that a prophet can temporarily suspend any norm of Jewish law but one: the injunction against idolatry. A true prophet cannot suspend the laws against idolatry, even temporarily ("Laws of the Foundations of the Torah" 9:5). Maimonides argued that unlike physics and metaphysics, which are esoteric disciplines requiring intellectual preparation and maturity and therefore not meant for the masses, knowledge of God's incorporeality must be revealed to the multitude. Teaching the masses about God's incorporeality is a halakhic imperative because "there is no profession of unity unless the doctrine of God's corporeality is denied" (*Guide* 1:35).

Maimonides was philosophically convinced that idolatry comprises not only how to worship but also, and even more important, our conception of whom to worship. False belief, that is, belief in divine corporeality, constitutes idolatry because instead of worshiping God, we thus worship a figment of the human imagination. Hence correct belief (philosophy) is crucial in order to identify God correctly and thus to avoid worshiping false gods (see Halbertal and Margalit, *Idolatry*).

The theme of idolatry is dealt with in two places in the *Mishneh Torah:* the "Laws of Idolatry," concerning pagan practices and influences, and the "Laws of the Foundations of the Torah," on the idolatry that can surface even within a halakhically defined way of life. Halakhah protects us from intermediary worship, the mistake of the early idol worshipers. "The essential principle in the precepts concerning idolatry is that we are not to worship any thing created— neither angel, sphere, star, none of the four elements, nor whatever has been formed from them. Even if the worshipper is aware that the Eternal is God, and worships the created thing in the sense in which Enosh and his contemporaries did, he is an idolater" ("Laws of Idolatry" 2:1). The laws of idolatry protect us from misguided forms of worship. Although the Jewish community has a halakhically defined way of worshiping God which distinguishes it from pagan nations, if Jews lack a philosophical understanding of God's otherness, idolatry will eventually reappear. Paganism can grow in Jewish halakhic soil if one does not understand how unity and incorporeality entail each other. Maimonides deals with this form of idolatry in the opening halakhoth of the *Mishneh Torah*.

> The basic principle of all basic principles and the pillar of all sciences is to realize that there is a First Being who brought every existing thing into being. All existing things, whether celestial, terrestrial, or belonging to an intermediate class, exist only through His true Existence.
>
> If it could be supposed that He did not exist, it would follow that nothing else could possibly exist.
>
> If, however, it were supposed that all other beings were nonexistent, He alone would still exist. Their non-existence would not involve His non-existence. For all beings are in need of Him; but He, blessed be He, is not in need of them nor of any of them.
>
> Hence, His real essence is unlike that of any of them.
>
> This is what the prophet means when he says "But the Eternal is the true God" (Jer. 10:10); that is, He alone is real, and nothing else has reality like His reality. The same thought the Torah expresses in the text: "There is none else besides Him" (Deut. 4:35); that is: there is no being besides Him, that is really like Him. This being is the God of the Universe, the Lord of all the Earth. And He it is, who controls the Sphere (of the Universe) with a power that is without end or limit; with a power that is never intermitted. For the Sphere is always revolving; and it is impossible for it to revolve without someone making it revolve. God, blessed be He, it is, who, without hand or body, causes it to revolve.

To acknowledge this truth is an affirmative precept, as it is said, "I am the Lord, thy God" (Ex. 20:2; Deut. 5:6). And whoever permits the thought to enter his mind that there is another deity besides this God, violates a prohibition; as it is said "Thou shalt have no other gods before me" (Ex. 20:3; Deut. 5:7), and denies the essence of Religion—this doctrine being the great principle on which everything depends.

This God is One. He is not two nor more than two, but One; so that none of the things existing in the universe to which the term one is applied is like unto His Unity; neither such a unit as a species which comprises many units (e.g. sub-species), nor such a unit as a physical body which consists of parts and dimensions. His Unity is such that there is no other Unity like it in the world. If there were plural deities, these would be physical bodies; because entities, that can be enumerated and are equal in their essence, are only distinguishable from each other by the accidents that happen to physical bodies. If the Creator were a physical body, He would have bounds and limits, for it is impossible for a physical body to be without limits; and where a body is limited and finite, its energy is also limited and finite. And our God, blessed be His Name, since His power is infinite and unceasing—for the Sphere (of the Universe) is continually revolving—His power is not the energy of a physical body. And since He is not a physical body, the accidents that happen to physical bodies do not apply to Him, so as to distinguish Him from another being. Hence, it is impossible that He can be anything but One. To realize this truth is an affirmative precept, as it is said "The Eternal, our God, is One God" (Deut. 6:4). ("Laws of the Foundations of the Torah" 1:1–7)

Thus Scholem's exaggerated criticism of Maimonides breaks down in the face of Maimonides' commitment to root out all vestiges of idolatry in the Jewish community.

I shall now consider a more basic critique of Maimonides, based on his neutralization of history as the framework of faith in the living God of Judaism. Unlike Halevi,

Maimonides interprets "I am the Lord, your God" without reference to "who brought you out of the land of Egypt, the house of bondage" (Exod. 20:2). One fulfills the positive commandment to know this God by understanding the concept of God as first being, necessary existent. The commandment to know God is fulfilled through philosophical reflection on the nature of being, which is independent of history. Halevi reflects the biblical emphasis on the events of history that proclaim the living God of Israel. As the biblical scholar and theologian Walther Zimmerli notes:

> "I am Yahweh, your God, who led you out of the land of Egypt, out of the house of slavery" (Exod. 20:2). This confession makes it clear that Israel did not derive her knowledge of God and, of course, the instructions of her God from a general belief in the creation; rather she is conscious that this knowledge is founded on a quite concrete encounter in the course of her history. . . . Israel knows her God from the experience of being saved. . . . It is this point of contact with the concrete events of history that distinguishes Israel's faith; it is a faith far removed from any relationship to God which derives from philosophical reflection. Old Testament faith is not conditioned by or directed to the beyond, to something in the background which stands over against the concrete course of history. It remains bound to the experiences of its own history both in song of praise and in revolt and knows that it is there that it meets its God. (*Old Testament and the World,* pp. 7–8)

The biblical scholar and theologian Moshe Greenberg suggested that chapter 20 of Ezekiel can be read as a classic example of the religious paradigm that informs Halevi's philosophy. According to the prophet, God's name is profaned "in the sight of the nations" when Israel is in exile, and therefore God promises to redeem Israel so that He "will be sanctified through you in the sight of the nations" (Ezek. 20:41). According to Ezekiel, God's redemptive actions on Israel's behalf are connected to His concern for His own dignity. Israel must be redeemed in order for God to be sanctified in the world.

Halevi, like Ezekiel and other biblical prophets, believed that God was revealed in the world through His role in Israel's history. The experiences of the people of Israel are crucial for realizing the kingdom of God in history. For Maimonides, however, God becomes accessible to humanity through creation, that is, through observation and rational speculation on His wisdom as it is manifest in the orderly patterns of nature.

What is there in the Jewish tradition that could have supported Maimonides' radical departure from the biblical worldview? If Judaism had consisted solely of the Bible, then his embrace of the God of the Philosophers would have been incomprehensible and the criticisms leveled against him for substituting nature for history justified. It is therefore important to bear in mind that observant religious Jews never viewed the Bible alone as the foundation of their faith. The rabbinic interpretive tradition was a much greater determinant of their religious consciousness than the Bible. And it must not be forgotten that Maimonides was the great master of the talmudic tradition. I shall now examine specific talmudic texts which suggest alternatives to the theology of miracles and historical events as the predominant representations of God's intimate relationship with Israel.

"R. Hillel said: There shall be no Messiah for Israel, because they have already enjoyed him in the days of Hezekiah. R. Joseph said: May God forgive him [for saying so]"

(T.B. Sanhedrin 99b). Notwithstanding Rashi's interpretation of Rabbi Hillel's point as "the Almighty will himself redeem Israel and reign over them," Rabbi Joseph's vehement reaction suggests that he understood Rabbi Hillel to mean that historical redemption was no longer essential for making sense of the Jewish tradition. For Rabbi Hillel, Judaism is a viable, living tradition independent of historical redemption. The commitment to the Sinai covenant does not entail a belief in the eventual messianic triumph of God in history. Although I am not claiming that Hillel's opinion was the accepted view of the rabbinic tradition, the Talmud was able to tolerate and include such a religious perspective.

There are several other rabbinic texts that indicate a rethinking of the notion of divine power in history. After witnessing the miraculous defeat of the Egyptians, the parting of the Reed Sea, and the deliverance of a powerless group of slaves, the prophet Moses leads Israel in a spontaneous victory song celebrating God's redemptive and triumphant power.

> I will sing to the Lord, for He has triumphed gloriously;
> Horse and driver He has hurled into the sea.
> The Lord is my strength and might;
> He is become my salvation.
> This is my God and I will enshrine Him;
> The God of my father, and I will exalt Him.
> The Lord, the Warrior—
> Lord is His name!
> Pharaoh's chariots and his army
> He has cast into the sea;
>
> .  .  .  .  .  .  .  .  .
>
> Your right hand, O Lord glorious in power,
> Your right hand, O Lord, shatters the foe!

In Your great triumph You break Your opponents;
You send forth Your fury, it consumes them like straw.

. . . . . . . . . . . . . . . . . .

Who is like You, O Lord, among the mighty;
Who is like You, majestic in holiness,
Awesome in splendor, working wonders! (Exod. 15:1–11)

"Who is like You, O Lord, among the mighty"? (*mi kamokha ba-'elim* ['*elim,* "mighty"]). Who can be compared to God, to the overwhelming might of the triumphant Lord of history? The song at the parting of the sea is full of praise for God's power to defeat Israel's enemies. The midrash (*Mekhilta,* tractate Shirata 8), however, offers a very different reading of these words of praise. In place of *mi kamokha ba-'elim ha-shem* it reads *mi kamokha ba-'ilmim ha-shem:* Who is like You, O Lord, among the silent ones? (*ilmim,* "mute, voiceless"). Who is like You who sees insult heaped upon Your children, yet remains silent? In place of the mighty assertive power of God in Egypt and at the Reed Sea the *Mekhilta* introduces us to God's silence and restraint. The victory and triumph of God in the Exodus story was not evident in Israel's exilic history, and therefore a new mode for understanding God's power in history was required.

This motif in the *Mekhilta* recurs as well in both the Babylonian and the Jerusalem Talmuds:

For R. Joshua b. Levi said: Why are they called men of the Great Assembly? Because they restored the crown of the divine attributes to its ancient completeness. [For] Moses had come and said: The great God, the mighty and the awesome God. Then Jeremiah came and said: Aliens are destroying His temple. Where, then, are His awesome deeds? Hence he omitted [the attribute] "awesome." Daniel came and said: Aliens are enslaving His sons.

Where are His mighty deeds? Hence he omitted the word "mighty." But they came and said: On the contrary! Therein lie His mighty deeds, that He suppresses His wrath, that He extends long-suffering to the wicked. Therein lie His awesome powers: For but for the fear of Him, how could one [single] nation persist among the [many] nations! But how could [the earlier] Rabbis abolish something established by Moses? R. Eleazer said: Since they knew that the Holy One, blessed be He, insists on truth, they would not ascribe false [things] to Him. (T.B. Yoma 69b)

Two prophets, Daniel and Jeremiah, each in some way change the traditional description of God because history no longer confirms His power and protective might. But then the rabbis of the great assembly respond by arguing that God's power is no longer expressed in victory and triumph but rather in defeat and forbearance. God's power is now manifest in divine silence and self-restraint. If you followed the Bible, you saw God's power in the defeat of Pharaoh's armies, in their drowning in the sea. But if you were a rabbinic Jew, like the author of the above midrash, you were taught to perceive God's power in divine reticence and restraint. The triumphant God of the Bible who vanquishes His enemies now waits patiently for the wicked to return. This clearly is a new understanding of God.

This descriptive haggadic motif also enters normative halakhic practice. The Talmud teaches that a person who sees a pagan temple should recite this blessing: "Our Rabbis taught: If one sees a statue of Hermes, he says, 'Blessed be He who shows long suffering to those who transgress His will'" (T.B. Berakhot 57b). Maimonides in the "Laws of Blessings" (10:9) codifies this injunction as law. Normative practice is thus also informed by the haggadic understanding of God's actions in history.

I am suggesting that this new understanding of divine power in both haggadic and halakhic contexts contains the seeds of a new religious sensibility. The emergence of this new sensibility takes many forms in rabbinic thought. One such text centers on the question of why God does not destroy the objects of idolatrous worship.

> Our Rabbis taught: Philosophers asked the elders in Rome, "If your God has no desire for idolatry, why does He not abolish it?" They replied, "If what is worshipped were something the world has no need of, He would abolish it; but people worship the sun, moon, stars and planets; should He destroy the Universe on account of fools! The world pursues its natural course (ʿolam k'minhago noheg) and as for the fools who act wrongly, they will have to render an account. Another illustration: Suppose a man stole a measure of wheat and went and sowed it in the ground; it is right that it should not grow (din hu shelo titzmah) but the world pursues its natural course and as for the fools who act wrongly, they will have to render an account. Another illustration: Suppose a man has intercourse with his neighbor's wife; it is right that she should not conceive (din hu shelo titʿabber), but the world pursues its natural course and as for the fools who act wrongly, they will have to render an account." This is similar to what R. Simeon b. Lakish said: "The Holy One, blessed be He, declared, Not enough that the wicked put coinage to vulgar use, but they trouble Me and compel Me to set My seal thereon!" (T.B. Avodah Zarah 54b)

Din hu shelo titzmah and din hu shelo titʿabber express our legitimate expectations that the world will reflect the revelatory will of the God of Sinai. On the other hand, ʿolam k'minhago noheg, "the world pursues its natural course," points to an impersonal, independent world that is not always responsive to our moral and theological intuitions. The tension in this gemara (talmudic text) results from an interesting juxtaposition of two perceptions of reward and punishment. A radical reading of the biblical text suggests an organic relationship between nature and mitzvah: "If, then, you obey the commandments that I enjoin upon you this day, loving the Lord your God and serving Him with all your heart and soul, I will grant the rain for your land in season, the early rain and the late. You shall gather in your new grain and wine and oil—I will also provide grass in the fields for your cattle—and thus you shall eat your fill" (Deut. 11:11). In the Bible, if you fulfill the commandments, the rains will come in time, your crops will grow, and you will prosper because nature and the mitzvah reflect the will and power of the same God.

In this kind of reading of the biblical promises of reward and punishment it is legitimate to expect nature not to co-operate with actions that violate the Torah. Adultery should not result in pregnancy; stolen grains should not take root and grow. Nonetheless, the talmudic discussion goes further than the reason given in the mishnah ("Should He destroy His universe on account of fools?") by adding the reason "the world pursues its natural course" ('olam k'minhago no-heg). According to the mishnah, God decides not to act so as not to destroy the world. This reason does not explain why stolen wheat grows and an adulterous woman conceives; if God were to prevent these actions the world would not be destroyed. For the gemara, God allows the natural world to pursue orderly patterns and therefore thieves, adulterers, and idolaters do not move Him to interfere and disrupt the inherent patterns of nature.

The talmudic discussion defers the judgment of the "fools" who defy God's will to a future time. Nevertheless we should not expect to see this judgment mirrored in the regular patterns of nature. God allows nature to operate in accordance with its own inherent structure independent of our moral and religious behavior. Although we can hope for the ultimate unity of revelation and physics, of mitzvah and biology, we must not confuse anticipation with present reality. Our understanding of the world now must acknowledge the empirical structures and constraints of nature. Even though the biblical promises of God's judgment are not given up but simply postponed, we must not expect to find reward and punishment in our daily lives. This bold postponement of the biblical world is expressed in the striking statement of Rabbi Jacob: "There is not a single commandment in the Torah whose reward is [stated] alongside it which is not dependent on the resurrection of the dead." The talmudic text mentions Rabbi Jacob's opinion in connection with the reward of long life that is promised in the Bible in connection with two commandments:

> Honor your father and your mother, as the Lord your God has commanded you, that you may long endure, and that you may fare well in the land that the Lord your God is assigning to you (Deut. 5:16);

and

> If, along the road, you chance upon a bird's nest, in any tree or on the ground, with fledglings or eggs and the mother sitting over the fledglings or on the eggs, do not take the mother together with her young. Let the mother go, and take the young, in order that you may fare well and have a long life. (Deut. 22:7)

The Talmud (T.B. Qiddushin 39b) relates the following incident: "Now, if someone's father said to him, 'Ascend to the loft and bring me young birds,' and he ascends to the loft, dismisses the mother bird and takes the young, and on returning falls and dies—where is this person's welfare and where is this person's prolonging of days? But 'that you may fare well' means in a world that is totally good; and 'that your days may be prolonged'—in a world that is totally prolonged." The talmudic discussion of this incident does not give up so quickly on the biblical promise of long life. "Now, perhaps there was no such occurrence?—R. Jacob witnessed such an incident. Then perhaps he was contemplating a transgression?—The Holy one, blessed be He, does not join an evil thought to a deed. But perhaps he was contemplating idolatry, and it is written, 'that I may take the house of Israel in their own heart' (Ezek. 14:5)?—That too was precisely his [Rabbi Jacob's] point: if you believe that commandments are rewarded in this world, then why did the commandments not protect such a person from having evil thoughts?" (T.B. Qiddushin 39b).

The Talmud struggles with the evidence and offers alternative explanations for the child's death that would not undermine a belief in the biblical promises. It is not easy to give up the conception of a world in which God assures us of the connection between observance of the commandments and the promise of long life and prosperity. Nevertheless, this talmudic text rejects all attempts to preserve the biblical worldview and accepts Rabbi Jacob's explanation, *sekhar mitzvah behai 'alma leka*, "there is no reward for commandments in this world." In other words, it is a mistake to bring the biblical worldview into our present historical reality.

How, one may ask, can a rabbinic teacher present a picture of the world that lacks the dramatic immediacy of the biblical notion of reward and punishment? Yehuda Halevi argued that the reality of divinity could be conveyed only through the living experience of the divine will acting in history. Yet the rabbinic texts under discussion give expression to a spiritual life with only faint echoes of this biblical paradigm. Here the empirical world does not always resonate in response to our observance of God's will. This, I believe, signifies a difficult yet fundamental shift away from biblical religious sensibilities. Although the texts in tractates Qiddushin and 'Avodah Zarah reveal a struggle to hold onto the biblical world by postponing biblical promises to some future time, they also indicate a bold willingness to rethink the whole religious approach to life.

To explain such a fundamental shift in religious sensibilities, we must try to understand what replaced the sense of certainty of God's presence that had been revealed in historical events. If, as Walther Zimmerli claimed, "Israel . . . is involved in a promise of the divine presence which will lead her in the events of the world in which she lives. . . . The theme of being with and leading the people dominates the whole of the Israel events with which the Old Testament, the book of the divine instruction of Israel, is concerned" (*Old Testament and the World,* pp. 9, 11), then in what is the presence of God revealed in rabbinic Judaism? Even though the biblical framework was not abandoned, there had to have been an alternative framework that mediated God as a continuous living presence.

Some Zionist historians claim that postbiblical Jews survived and were sustained by the dream of one day returning to Israel. I cannot believe, however, that a people could have persisted in a state of repression and postponed gratification for two thousand years. And I doubt that the Jewish people survived only because they trusted in the eventual appearance of the messiah and an end to their exile. There must have been something in their immediate circumstances that compensated for God's silence.

Although they constructed imaginative haggadic narratives to support their belief that one day God would vindicate Israel, I am convinced that something else besides messianism served as the carrier of the living God in their everyday lives. And that, I suggest, was the shift in the tradition from an event-based to a text-centered theology. The Torah, as the word of God, became a substitute for events as carriers of the living God. God, as it were, became incarnate in the words of the Torah. In meditation on the Torah, God's presence was felt because God's word was alive and compelling. "When ten people sit together and occupy themselves with the Torah, the Shekhinah (divine presence) abides among them, as it is said: 'God stands in the godly congregation.' (Ps. 82:1) Whence do we know that the same applies even to five? . . . Whence do we know that the same applies even to three? . . . Whence do we know that the same applies even to two? . . . Whence do we know that the same applies even to one? It is said: 'In every place where I have My name mentioned I will come to you and bless you'" (Mishnah Avot 3:7).

The crucial point was that divinity no longer revealed itself exclusively through events. Jews didn't read the equivalent of the *New York Times* to discover signs of God's redemptive actions. They opened up the Torah and by study and analysis felt that they were engaging Him directly. One cannot but notice the sense of joy and the complete involvement with the Torah in the daily prayers Jews recited. "Blessed art thou, Lord our God, King of the universe, who has sanctified us with thy commandments and commanded us to study the Torah. May the words of the Torah, Lord our God, be sweet in our mouth and in the mouth of all Your people so that we, our children, and all the children of the House of Israel may come to know You and to study Your Torah with selfless devotion. Blessed art thou, O Lord, who teaches the Torah to His people Israel" (daily morning service).

In the study of the Torah one engages God not as the lord of history but as a loving teacher. One sensed God's continuous love by one's immersion in the words of the Torah. It is as if the revelation of the Torah at Sinai, where God is midrashically portrayed as a teacher, absorbs the triumphant lord of history of the Exodus narrative. The Torah becomes the new channel for experiencing God's immediacy. This experience is beautifully expressed in the following prayer: "You have loved the house of Israel Your people with everlasting love; You have taught us the Torah and mitzvoth, laws and judgments. Therefore, Lord our God, when we lie down and when we rise up we will speak of Your laws, and rejoice in the words of Your Torah and in Your mitzvoth for evermore. Indeed, they are our life and the length of our days; we will meditate on them day and night. May You never take away Your love from us. Blessed are You, O Lord, who loves Your people Israel" (daily evening service).

This idea is not an exclusively rabbinic innovation; even in Psalm 119 God and the word of God are practically interchangeable. In Psalm 119 it is not always clear whether the author is referring to the word of God or to God as such.

As C. A. Briggs points out, "The psalmist is entirely loyal to the Law. The Law has become to him the representative of his God. Throughout the psalm he ascribes to the Law the attributes older writers ascribe to God; looks to the Law for the help and salvation that ordinarily come from God alone" (*A Critical and Exegetical Commentary on the Book of Psalms,* p. 417). One of the most revealing parts of this psalm, as Moshe Greenberg and Yohanan Muffs have pointed out, is verse 48: *Ve-'esah kappai 'el mitzvotekha 'asher 'ahavti ve-'asikha be-huqqekha"* (I lift up my hands to your commandments which I have loved, I study your statutes). In the Book of Lamentations we find, *shifkhi khamayim libech, nokhah penei 'adonai; se'i 'elav kappayyikh 'al nefesh 'olalayyikh* (Pour out your heart like water before the face of the Lord; lift up your hands [*se'i kappayyikh*] toward him for the life of your young children; 2:19). The same terminology (*se'i kappayyikh/'esah kappai*) is used to refer to a turn to God in prayer (Lamentations) and to the commandments (Psalms 119).

It is interesting to observe how different biblical scholars interpret this psalm. Greenberg, who was trained and nurtured by both the biblical and rabbinic traditions, writes:

> There is a new religiosity in this psalm. Religious sentiment, religious emotion—love, delight, clinging to—are now focused on the Torah, the Teaching, but God is not therewith displaced; on the contrary, the entire psalm is addressed to God. "You" in the psalm is God, and "your Torah," "your precepts," "your commandments," are praised. The Torah does not come between the psalmist and God; it serves to link them. God's Torah, his commandments, rules, precepts, testimonies, words—all these are available on earth to the religious Israelites, enabling them at all times to feel contact with God. God's presence is assured within

the human community through his Torah that he has bestowed on Israel. The closeness to God through preoccupation with Torah is regarded by the psalmist as the most precious experience he can have: through meditation on the Torah, through the love of [it], and the clinging to it, to feel the presence of God. ("Three Conceptions of the Torah in Hebrew Scriptures," p. 21)

Arthur Weiser, who reflects the Christian emphasis on salvation and grace in which religious passion is nurtured by God's redemptive actions in history and by the anticipation of a new redemptive breakthrough in the future, responds differently to the religious implications of this psalm.

It is possible to deduce from the psalm a full-fledged "theology" of law, in both its theoretical and its practical aspects. The simple form of the diction makes it unnecessary to expound the psalm in detail. It only remains to point out that the kind of piety, based on the law, such as is presented to us in the psalm does not yet exhibit that degeneration and hardening into a legalistic form of religion to which it succumbed in late Judaism and which provoked Jesus' rebuke. On the other hand, however, one cannot fail to realize that a piety such as is expressed in the psalm, according to which God's word and law take the place of God himself and his wondrous works (v. 13), are even worshiped (v. 48) and become the source of the comfort which as a rule is bestowed upon man by the divine saving grace (vv. 50, 92), carries with it the germs of a development which was bound to end in the self-righteousness of the Pharisees and scribes. (*Old Testament Library: The Psalms,* p. 740)

Weiser fails to appreciate the religious intimacy and divine love that Jews discovered in the study of the Torah and in living by the mitzvoth. To him, rabbinic culture is a legalism that must degenerate into "the self-righteousness of the Pharisees and scribes." It appears that at a crucial moment in history two alternative spiritual ways emerged from the biblical tradition. One focused on the Exodus in terms of the longing for salvation, the other on the moment of Sinai in which the Torah and mitzvoth mediate God's presence.

One can argue that the religious perception of God in Psalm 119 infuses rabbinic culture as a whole. One can sense God's continuous love when meditating day and night on the Torah. The mitzvoth mediate divine love. Revelation is reenacted continuously through the continuous engagement with the word of God. There is never a sense of what Martin Buber called the "eclipse of God" because so long as the Torah is present, God is present.

Rabbinic Judaism developed a new paradigm that differed from the dominant biblical model. I believe that had Jews retained the biblical framework alone they would have gone insane. An event-based theology would have driven then into collective manic-depression. Victory suggests "God loves me"; defeat, "God has withdrawn His love." What saved them from this manic-depressive relationship with God was a text-centered theology that made God's presence in history a function of the presence of the Torah. As long as we were the carriers of learning and continued to interpret God's word, God was present. In addition to the central significance given to the study of the Torah, the presence of God was felt in all aspects of life because of the expanded range of halakhic obligation.

Although the rabbis did not abandon the belief in historical redemption, their daily religious lives were not fueled by messianism. The crucial issues characterizing a religious culture are not necessarily questions of dogma and doctrinal belief: Do you believe in messianism? Do you pray for the restoration of the sacrificial cult? When Maimonides was asked, "Do you believe in the resurrection of the dead?" he answered truthfully and without hesitation: "Yes." And had he been further challenged by the leading question, "If, as you claim, the soul can achieve immortality immediately after bodily death and become engaged in timeless contemplation, what sense is there to wanting to return to a bodily form of existence? How can you, Maimonides, believe in the resurrection of the dead?" Maimonides would have responded by saying (as he did in his "Essay on the Resurrection of the Dead"): "I believe in this doctrine because of tradition. So long as it is not logically absurd, I accept the traditional belief."

The question of the religious significance or function of beliefs is a different matter. Maimonides could well have continued, "I believe in miracles. As I wrote in the *Guide,* if God were to will it, God could destroy the world. God can change the nature of anything. But as a matter of fact, God doesn't." This clarification marks the difference between a spiritual life according to Maimonides and one according to Yehuda Halevi. The important issue in religious life is not which dogma you accept but what serves as the catalyst of your religious soul. What organizes your spiritual identity? What beliefs carry and enliven you as a spiritual person? Is it the anticipation of a triumphant God of history or your engagement in Torah learning and halakhic observance?

I claim that because Maimonides was a great talmudist he was able to appropriate Aristotle. If he had had only the Bible, then he would have found Athens and Jerusalem irreconcilable. The prophet versus the philosopher; Moses versus Aristotle. In Jerusalem you heard one lecture, in

Athens a very different one. In Jerusalem, you heard about God parting the sea, raining manna on the desert, and drawing water out of rocks. The power of God becomes visible in the Bible to the degree that Israel's complete dependency on Him becomes evident. Gideon refuses to have a large, strong army because only a small force could highlight the power of God (Judges 7). Israel's weakness in Egypt and in the desert serves as a transparent symbol of God's providential power.

In the rabbinic tradition, however, God is revealed through the empowerment of human beings to uncover and expand the meaning of the Torah through rational reflection and legal argumentation. The Talmud gave precedence to the interpretation of the Torah by scholars over the direct revelation of the Torah by God. There is a well-known haggadic story involving a dispute among talmudic sages about the ritual status of the "oven of Aknai." Rabbi Eliezer declared it ritually pure; the sages argued that it was impure. After failing to convince the sages through rational arguments, Rabbi Eliezer then invoked miracles to convince his colleagues. Seeing that the sages still did not accept his position despite the miraculous "hints" of divine support, Rabbi Eliezer tried to present what might be considered the final knock-out blow in any argument involving the interpretation of the Torah: God's direct intervention in support of his point of view.

> Again he said to them: "if the law is as I say, let it be proved from heaven!" Whereupon a heavenly voice cried out: "Why do you dispute with Rabbi Eliezer, seeing that in all matters the law is as he says!" But Rabbi Joshua arose and exclaimed: "It is not in heaven" [Deut. 30.12]. What did he mean by this? Said Rabbi Jeremiah: "That the Torah had already been given at Mount Sinai; we

pay no attention to a heavenly voice, because Thou has long since written in the Torah at Mount Sinai, 'After the majority must one incline' " [Exod. 23.2]. Rabbi Nathan met Elijah and asked him: "What did the Holy One, blessed be He, do at that moment?" He replied: "He laughed, saying: 'My children have defeated me, My children have defeated Me.' " (T.B. Baba Metzia 59b)

Rabbinic Judaism loosened the grip of the biblical paradigm by lessening the need for revelation. There is a classic talmudic text that clearly implies that from the death of Moses onward the role of prophets and the appeal to revelation became irrelevant to problems of ascertaining the correct understanding of the Torah. The Talmud states that many laws were forgotten during the period of mourning for Moses. The principle "It is not in heaven" was repeatedly invoked in order to show that revelation was no longer available as a way to rediscover those forgotten laws. "Rav Judah reported in the name of Samuel: Three thousand traditional laws were forgotten during the period of mourning for Moses. They said to Joshua: 'Ask'; he replied: 'It is not in heaven' (Deut. 30:12). They [the Israelites] said to Samuel: 'Ask'; he replied: [Scripture says:] 'These are the commandments' (Num 36:3) implying [that since the promulgation of these commandments] no prophet has now the right to introduce anything new" (T.B. Temurah 16a). After listing several incidents where Pinhas and Joshua sought in vain to rediscover forgotten laws by appealing directly to God, the Talmud asserts in the name of Rabbi Abbuha that even though thousands of legal teachings were forgotten during the period of mourning for Moses, "Othniel, the son of Kenaz, restored [these forgotten teachings] as a result of dialectics" (T.B. Temurah 16a). Human beings can, through their own reasoning, compensate for the absence of God's active involvement in revealing the Torah. Learning, not just direct revelation, is a source of the word of God.

The absence of revelation is not a tragedy as long as there are scholars who can restore the full content and scope of the Torah by their intellectual efforts. What is more, greater credibility is granted to those whose authority is based on their own intellectual competence than to prophets who are the mouthpiece of God. "They [the scribes and the prophets] are like two agents whom a king sent to a province. With regard to one, he wrote: 'If he show you my signature and seal, trust him, but otherwise do not trust him.' With regard to the other, he wrote: 'Even if he does not show you my signature and seal, trust him.' So of the words of prophecy, it is written: 'If there arises in the midst of you a prophet . . . and he gives you a sign' (Deut. 13:2); but of the words of the scribes it is written: 'According to the law which they shall teach you' (Deut. 17:11)" (Song of Songs Rabbah 1:2).

The prophet—the paradigmatic mediator between God and human beings in the case of the written Torah—appeals to direct revelation; he addresses the community in the name of God, and his legitimacy is conditional on his ability to produce proof of his direct contact with God (signs and miracles are the signature and seal of God). The scribes and scholars of the talmudic tradition gain authority by virtue of the "law which they teach," that is, intellectual competence to reason and argue cogently about the law.

Maimonides can thus be said to have followed rabbinic precedents, such as those discussed previously, when he rejected history as the exclusive framework for a spiritual way of life. He went further, however, in extending the principle that sets constraints on the religious imagination from the legal, halakhic world to the study of nature. For Maimonides, nature and being—what was known through the study of physics and metaphysics—played the role that the Torah did in the talmudic tradition. It is not surprising therefore that Maimonides in the *Mishneh Torah* made the bold move of including *pardes* studies, that is, physics and metaphysics, within the rubric of *talmud*, thus placing these disciplines within the traditional conception of Torah studies.

> The time allotted to study should be divided into three parts. A third should be devoted to the Written Law; a third to the Oral Law; and the last third should be spent in reflection, deducing conclusions from premises, developing implications of statements, comparing dicta, studying the hermeneutical principles by which the Torah is interpreted, till one knows the essence of these principles, and how to deduce what is permitted and what is forbidden from what one has learnt traditionally. This is termed Talmud. . . . The words of the Prophets are comprised in the Written Law, while their exposition falls within the category of the Oral Law. The subjects styled *Pardes* (Esoteric Studies), are included in *Talmud*. ("Laws of the Study of the Torah" 1:11–12)

The divine presence is mediated through natural science and metaphysics. Although the medium shifts from revelation to the Torah to the study of nature, there is a fundamental similarity in the movement away from historical events in both the rabbinic and the Maimonidean framework of spirituality. The difference between them is the different frames of reference of their spiritual concerns. For Maimonides, only pardes studies can give the constancy of divine presence that rabbinic culture sought to create.

I believe that the movement away from dependency on

divine responsiveness and temporal reward and punishment was a safeguard against the allure of "alien gods" who promised the material blessings of this world. The Torah, as the revelation of God's presence, rescued Jews from changing their faith to the various gods of history who offered promises of security and well-being.

Rabbinic Judaism showed us that as long as we have access to God in our everyday lives, we have less need for victory and divine intervention. We became victors in the *beit midrash* (academy of learning). As long as we had the beit midrash and leaders like Yohanan ben Zakai who were prepared to say to the Romans during their siege of Jerusalem, "Give me the city of Yavneh and its scholars," we could live without Jerusalem and the Temple. One does not need to control history as long as one controls the text. One does not require revelation and prophecy when scholars are available to offer rational legal arguments. And with this text-centered paradigm of dignity, freedom, and control, Jews moved from a biblical to a rabbinic culture, even, in the case of Maimonides, to a philosophical culture.

Halevi, whose sensibility was basically biblical, had difficulty acknowledging the power of human rationality and talmudic legal argumentation to represent the word of God. According to Halevi, the Mishnah derives its authority from the presence of *ruah ha-qodesh*, "the holy spirit." "The conciseness of its speech, the beauty of its structure, and the excellence of its composition, encompassing [all] aspects of the meanings [they discussed] authoritatively and decisively without [succumbing to] doubt and conjecture, is at such a point that anyone who considers it with an eye for the truth will see that human beings [simply] fall short of composing anything like it unless it is with divine assistance" (*Kuzari* 3:67). The authority and certainty of prophecy—the central category of biblical religion—infuses Halevi's interpretation of talmudic Halakhah. For him rabbinic legislation makes sense and is authoritative only if you believe that its authors, the rabbis of the Mishnah and the Talmud, were in some way divinely inspired (see *Kuzari* 3:41).

Jews recite the blessing "Who sanctified us with His mitzvoth and commanded us . . ." when lighting the candles on Hanukkah or reading the megillah on Purim, even though these postbiblical holidays were instituted after prophecy had ceased. The rabbis drew attention to the problematic nature of these references to God's command when they asked rhetorically: *"ve hechan zivanu?"* (And where did He command us?). Their answer suggests that rabbinic legislative authority can mediate the commanding presence of God. "R. Awai said: [It follows] from 'You shall act in accordance with the instructions given you and the ruling handed down to you; you must not deviate from the verdict that they announce to you either to the right or to the left' (Deut. 17:11). R. Nehemiah quoted: 'Remember the days of old, Consider the years of ages past; Ask your father, he will inform you, Your elders, they will tell you' (Deut 32:7). (T.B. Shabbat 23a). For Halevi, however, this is not sufficient. A legally argued interpretation cannot satisfy his need for the certainty and immediacy of divine revelation. He demands further reassurance that God was directly involved in determining the content of the legislative process in order to validate the expression "Who commanded us."

We are ordered to obey the authorized judge in every generation. . . . [Scripture] associated disobeying the priest and the judge with the very greatest crimes. . . . [That was the procedure to be followed] as long as the [traditional] system, consisting of the [sacrificial] service, the Sanhedrin, and the other groups through which the system was perfected, would remain intact, and [while] the divine order (*al-amr al-ilahi*) would undoubtedly be attached to them, either through prophecy or through support and inspiration, just as it was during the [period of] the Second Temple (T.B. Yoma 9b). . . . That is why the commandment [to read from] the Scroll of Esther and [to observe] Purim as well as the commandment [to observe] Hannukah became obligatory, and also [why] we were permitted to say [in benedictions recited before fulfilling these obligations], . . . "and who has commanded us to read the Scroll [of Esther]" and "to kindle the light of Hanukkah," "to complete the Hallel," "to recite [the Hallel]," "to wash the hands," [to observe] the commandment of the eruv," and other things besides [these]. If they were [merely] customs that arose after the Exile, they would surely not have been designated as "statutory," and it would not have been necessary for us [to recite] a benediction in connection with them]. (*Kuzari* 3:39)

Halevi thus collapses the oral tradition into the written tradition. The Mishnah and Talmud are assimilated into the biblical framework, where authority derives directly and solely from the word of God.

It is interesting to observe that in the *Kuzari* (3:53) Halevi uses the same type of argument against the Karaites who rejected the talmudic tradition as he used against the philosophers.

It is clear from this that there is no [way of] coming close to God except by [fulfilling] God's ordinances, exalted be He; and there is no way to the knowledge of God's ordinances, except by way of prophecy, [certainly] not by means of reasoning with one another and engaging in intellectual speculation. There is no connection

between us and those ordinances [revealed to the prophets], except by means of reliable tradition. Moreover, those who have
transmitted those laws to us were not just single individuals, but
rather a great many people as well as scholars, people of stature,
and [others] who had contact with the prophets.

Halevi's basic claim is that not only is revelation, rather
than reason and reflection, the only way to knowledge of
God, but that only the uninterrupted tradition that began
at Sinai can guarantee revelation. Consequently, the whole
rabbinic tradition, including its legal controversies and legislative boldness, is understood within the same revelatory
framework that makes Sinai the source of religious certainty.
A person loyal to the rabbinic tradition acquires a "healthy
reassurance about his Law, because it is handed down by a
chain of reliable authorities [about whom we may be confi-
dent] that their knowledge is from God, exalted be He. For
indeed, [even] if the Karaite's personal zeal were to attain
all that {it could conceivably attain}, he would still not get
any such reassurance [because of it], since he knows that his
personal zeal is [really a matter of] rationalizing and judging
arbitrarily. Therefore, he will not be confidant that his actions are pleasing to God, exalted be He" (*Kuzari* 3:50). The
themes of creation and revelation are central to Halevi and
Maimonides. Both thinkers posit the notion of divine will
in addition to divine wisdom. There is an important difference, however, in how they understand and apply the will
of God as manifest in creation and revelation.

For Halevi, creation primarily expresses the will of God
that becomes known to Adam through personal experience.
The will of God operates in the world after Creation in the
ongoing drama of divine intervention in history (see *Kuzari*

1:25). Maimonides, like Halevi, believed in the importance of the doctrine of Creation. In the *Guide of the Perplexed,* Maimonides argued at length that Aristotle had not presented proof for the eternity of the universe. Maimonides was careful, however, to articulate a position that accepted the doctrine of Creation without undermining the general philosophical framework of Aristotelian physics.

> The matter has now become clear to you and the doctrine epitomized. Namely we agree with Aristotle with regard to one half of his opinion and we believe that what exists is eternal a parte post and will last forever with that nature which He, may He be exalted, has willed; that nothing in it will be changed in any respect unless it be in some particular of it miraculously—although, He, may He be exalted, has the power to change the whole of it, or to annihilate it, or to annihilate any nature in it that He wills. However, that which exists has had a beginning, and at first nothing at all existed except God. His wisdom required that He should bring creation into existence at the time when He did do it, and that what He has brought into existence should not be annihilated nor any of its natures changed except in certain particulars that He willed to change; about some of these we know, whereas about others that will be changed in the future we do not know. This is our opinion and the basis of our Law. Aristotle, on the other hand, thinks that just as the world is eternal a parte post and will not pass away, it is also eternal a parte ante and has not been produced. (*Guide* 2:29)

For Maimonides, Creation was a founding rather than a controlling moment in Judaism. One begins with "will" but moves to "wisdom." One begins with miracle but moves to structure and order. Maimonides did not subscribe to an apocalyptic vision of history. For Maimonides, messianism is a moment within human history. Its exceptional nature is merely the result of changed political, economic, and social conditions that facilitate our capacity to know and love God. "The ultimate and perfect reward, the final bliss which will suffer neither interruption nor diminution is the life in the world to come. The Messianic era, on the other hand, will be realized in this world; which will continue in its normal course (*'olam k'minhago holekh*) except that independent sovereignty will be restored to Israel" ("Laws of Repentance" 9:2).

Messianism is an aspirational norm for history. The concept of the end of history or of the radical transformation of human nature is foreign to Maimonides' thinking. Messianic reality, as he describes it, could come about, persist for a period of time, and then cease to exist. Because he refused to accept religious doctrines predicated on a radical change in human nature, Maimonides understood Ezekiel's metaphor of a "new heart"—"And I will give you a new heart and put a new spirit into you: I will remove the heart of stone from your body and give you a heart of flesh; and I will put My spirit into you. Thus I will cause you to follow My laws and faithfully to observe My rules" (Ezekiel 36:26–27)—to mean: "For in those days, knowledge, wisdom and truth will increase, as it is said 'For the earth will be full of the knowledge of the Lord' (Is. 11:9), and it is said, 'They will no more teach everyone his neighbor' (Jer. 31:34), and further, 'I will remove the heart of stone from your flesh' (Ezek. 36:26). Because the King who will arise from the seed of David will possess more wisdom than Solomon and will be a great prophet, approaching Moses, our teacher, he will teach the whole of the Jewish people and instruct them in the way of God" ("Laws of Repentance" 9:2).

Maimonides emphasized repeatedly that the central implication of messianism was the permanence of the law. Nothing in the law will be changed when the Messiah arrives. This view can be understood not only as a polemic against Christianity but as an expression of Maimonides' conviction that the constancy of the law, if understood correctly, acts as a corrective to utopian politics. The emphasis on natural order and structure counteracts the belief that "will"—as concept and metaphor—creates a religious world in which everything is possible.

Halevi and Maimonides differ with regard to the role of the prophet and prophecy in interpreting and legislating the law after Moses. In *Kuzari* (3:41), Halevi does not accept Maimonides' position that there can be no prophetic legislation after Moses. For Halevi prophets after Moses may introduce new legislation that is not present in the Bible. For Maimonides, however, a prophet who cites prophecy to introduce new legislation or to interpret Mosaic legislation becomes thereby a false prophet who deserves death ("Laws of the Foundations of the Torah" 9:1). For Maimonides revelation as a source of God's legislative will is a founding moment; it ceased after Moses came down from Sinai.

We can draw an analogy between Maimonides' approach to prophecy within the context of rabbinic jurisprudence and his treatment of Creation. Just as Creation is considered a founding rather than a controlling moment in our understanding of reality, so too is prophecy—the embodiment and pristine expression of divine will—with regard to postbiblical rabbinic Judaism. The principle of will is absorbed by wisdom—human rationality—in the interpretative tradition. What Aristotelian physics is to the story of Creation, the talmudic interpretive tradition is to the revealed word of God.

The distinction between *a parte ante* and *a parte post,* which makes Aristotelian physics the operative framework of human knowledge of the world after Creation, can also be applied to the framework of legal argumentation and decision making that constitutes rabbinic Judaism. In the Talmud as Maimonides understood it, divine revelation is collapsed into the structures and categories of human reasoning and analysis. The prophet who appeals to prophecy in a legal discussion is ipso facto a false prophet. Prophets may not interfere in the normal processes of interpretation. Just as the anticipation of miracles does not define the structure of nature after Creation, so too prophets do not define the interpretive framework of Torah law *a parte post,* that is, after Sinai, when prophecy ceases to be the operative principle of Judaism.

Maimonides was prepared to collapse revelation into the rational human enterprise of learning and understanding whereas Halevi insisted that the prophetic mode is a continuous source of law. Hanukkah and Purim, though postbiblical and seemingly postprophetic, were for Halevi the result of divine inspiration.

Maimonides was not the Hellenic Aristotelian Harry Wolfson described in his early writings or the confused intellectual who according to Isaac Husik did not understand the difference between biblical prophets and philosophers. Maimonides understood philosophers as well as he understood the Bible. He believed, however, that the Bible was not the only source of Jewish spirituality, that there was also a living interpretive culture mediated by human understanding in which the scholar was greater than the prophet.

Notwithstanding the important differences between the biblical and rabbinic orientations to history and revelation, both shaped Jewish religious consciousness. The canonization of the twenty-four books of the Bible to include Proverbs, Ecclesiastes, and Job as well as the prophetic books like Isaiah, Jeremiah, and Ezekiel suggests that no one single theme defines authentic Judaism. The tradition was wise in allowing many different voices to speak within it. Different generations and individuals thus found room for their particular moral and religious sensibilities. Any attempt by scholars to decide whether Halevi or Maimonides truly reflects the Jewish tradition becomes in the end a confused and misguided undertaking.

There are many conflicting themes in both the biblical and the rabbinic traditions. In claiming that Maimonides reflects the rabbinic tradition, therefore, I am suggesting only that there are themes within rabbinic culture that can be understood as supporting his attempt to integrate a philosophical religious worldview within Judaism. Similarly, in asserting that Yehuda Halevi's philosophy of Judaism reflects biblical thought, I am suggesting only that his thinking is closer in spirit to the prophetic books of the Bible than to those currents in talmudic culture that minimize the importance of history and prophecy for the ongoing development of Judaism.

# CHAPTER FIVE

# Halakhic Sobriety and Inclusiveness

Modern Jewish consciousness has been deeply shaped by the dramatic events of recent Jewish history. The drama surrounding the Six-Day War, which was an important catalyst in reawakening Jewish self-awareness, testifies to the power of events in shaping Jewish identity. My own decision to leave the diaspora, to give up the security and economic comfort my family and I had enjoyed in Montreal and to take up residence and build a new life in Israel, was not only the result of intellectual reflection. The events preceding the Six-Day War awakened me to the power of Jewish solidarity throughout the world. I cannot forget the fear of another Holocaust that gripped many Jews before the war. Theologians suggested in all seriousness that we turn to the Book of Jeremiah to prepare Jews for another genocide. I recall my brother, who lived in Israel, telling me that thirty thousand graves were dug in Bnei Brak in anticipation of what might happen. I remember the strong sense of being unable to function normally because of my anxiety over the fate of Israeli society.

As a congregational rabbi and teacher of Jewish philosophy at McGill University, I remember the sudden sense of awakening diaspora Jews felt at the powerful drama of Jewish history that was now unfolding. Masses of people lined up at Jewish Federations prepared to give up their life's savings to help the war effort. Academics who had previously kept their connection with Judaism and the Jewish community hidden approached me and asked whether they could help by driving trucks or filling sandbags in Israel. I could hardly hide my surprise at their wanting to participate in the Jewish drama. And they too could not explain their feelings, even to themselves. The intensity of the event, of the historical moment, moved people in a way that defied rational comprehension. At that moment my family and I realized that our future could not be in North America when the fate of the Jewish people was being determined by what was taking place in Israel.

It might appear strange to argue for the importance of Maimonides and the Talmud, rather than of Halevi, to an appreciation of modern Judaism and the religious significance of the rebirth of the state of Israel. The early Zionist rejection of talmudic culture and its choice of the Promised Land as the place to implement its revolution suggests that biblical categories of thought and history are more fruitful keys to understanding the spiritual significance of Israel. An event-based theology like that of the Bible or of Halevi seems more in keeping with the modern Jewish experience. How can Maimonides' emphasis on the intellect as defining the essence of a human being and on the centrality of the studies of physics and metaphysics (*pardes*) in leading us to a passionate love and awe of God provide a viable vision of Judaism for a people absorbed by the drama of history?

The Six-Day War taught me that a deep part of me agreed with certain features of Halevi's understanding of Judaism. Nevertheless, I also vividly recall the extreme emotional change from the elation over the victory to the despair and anxiety that gripped the country during and after the Yom Kippur War. Although I still acknowledged the power of events, I now recognize the manic-depressive consequences possible in an event-grounded theology. I am drawn to the intellectual sobriety of Maimonides and of the talmudic tradition as ways of moderating the event-driven passions of traumatic historical events.

The rabbinic tradition's focus on Torah study and its all-embracing halakhic way of life counterbalance the significance of events for an understanding of God's relationship to Israel. Maimonides' emphasis on nature and the ahistorical character of his philosophical quest for God, like the talmudic emphasis on the study of the Torah, can empower us to withstand not only the idolatrous appeals of the false gods of history but also the devastating psychological effects of an event-based theology. Moving the goal of mitzvah observance beyond reward and punishment to the idea that "the reward of a mitzvah is the mitzvah," and using Torah study to illuminate our understanding of God's presence in history contribute to the sobriety and stability of a spiritual life. Maimonides and the Talmud lessen our vulnerability to the triumphant gods of history, be they conquering armies, nationalism, materialism, or whatever the modern equivalents are of the biblical God who promises well-being and security in exchange for obedience.

In the Middle Ages, Maimonides was criticized for undermining the unique importance of the Halakhah. Maimonides claimed that passionate love for God was accessible to all human beings through the study of nature, so why, the criticism went, should Jews suffer and make extreme sacrifices for the halakhic way of worshiping God? The modern equivalent to this medieval argument would be, if a person can live an ethical and fulfilling life outside a Jewish religious framework, what is special about Judaism? If we can find spiritual refinement and a path to God through art, music, literature, and other forms of human culture, why should we make such efforts to continue the Jewish tradition? The typical response to this critique is Halevi's argument that the rituals of Judaism and study of the Torah unleash spiritual powers that alone make communion with God possible. The contemporary fascination with Kabalistic approaches to Judaism and to religious beliefs ascribing cosmic significance to mitzvoth (an idea that recalls Gershom Scholem's claim that Halakhah becomes compelling only when ritual is understood as sacrament) is often driven by the need to discover the uniqueness of the Jewish people and the Jewish way of life.

Many Jewish theologians and rabbinic teachers believe that religious passion must be fueled by the nonrational, numinous features of Judaism. The only way to provide an attractive alternative to the secularism of the modern world is to emphasize the separation of Jewish religious life from everyday human experience. Judaism must be "radically other" and driven by its own distinctive logic in order to defeat the pragmatic emphases of modern secular culture. Cultural distinctiveness and separation from the world are necessary to strengthen Jewish religious identity.

The modern threat that Jews might be absorbed by the majority secular culture affects the importance we ascribe to symbolic rituals. Those who fear Jewish assimilation emphasize ritual over ethics in order to highlight the distinct way of life that characterizes the Jewish family. The secular expression of this preoccupation with uniqueness can be seen in the way the Holocaust is used to emphasize the distinctiveness of Jewish suffering and destiny. It is often considered a desecration to compare any other people's suffering with that of the Jews in the Holocaust.

Although I can understand the obsession with uniqueness as a reaction to the fear of Jewish assimilation and disappearance ("Will my grandchildren be Jewish?"), I nevertheless believe that we distort the meaning of Judaism as a way of life when we equate uniqueness with significance. In referring to the prevailing notions of universal human psychology to explain revelation, Maimonides interpreted the purpose of mitzvoth in terms of their value in producing and sustaining moral health. That there are other ways of creating a healthy human psyche may undermine the uniqueness of Jewish law but not its significance and value.

One of the gifts of living in Israel and of building a completely Jewish society is in no longer having to choose between ethics and ritual as the basis of our Jewish identity. In becoming "a nation like all other nations," Israel should have liberated us from our preoccupation with uniqueness. When I would teach Israeli soldiers about Leviticus 19, which enjoins Jews to pay workers' wages on time, not to hate others in their heart, not to take advantage of human weaknesses, and the like, I was surprised and disturbed by the following reaction: "All decent societies recognize these values. Why do you consider them necessary for building a Jewish society? I can live this way as a Norwegian or as a Dane. What makes this unique to the Jewish people and to Israel?" Apparently, it takes a long time to stop equating meaningfulness with uniqueness.

As I argued in my chapters on Halevi and Maimonides, one of the fundamental differences between the two is that for Halevi the history of Israel and of revelation are the points of departure for understanding Creation. Communion with God is linked to the divine gift God gave to Adam at the moment of Creation. This spiritual capacity eventually became the exclusive property of the community of Israel. In this way Halevi could explain the significance of Leviticus, with its detailed emphasis on animal sacrifices and ritual purity and impurity. What appears absurd from a rational perspective now becomes vital for achieving communion with God and nurturing this spiritual capacity.

We notice a similar tendency to interpret the Creation story in light of Israel's particular history in Rashi's commentary on the first verse of Genesis.

> "In the beginning" (Gen. 1:1): Rabbi Isaac said: It was not necessary to begin the Torah, [whose main object is to teach commandments, mitzvoth, with this verse] but from "This month shall be unto you" [the beginning of months] (Ex. 12:2) since this is the first mitzvah that Israel was commanded [to observe]. And what is the reason that it begins with Genesis? Because of [the verse] "The power of His works He hath declared to His people in giving them the heritage of the nations" (Ps. 111:6). For if the

nations of the world should say to Israel: "You are robbers, because you have seized by force the lands of the seven nations" [of Canaan], they [Israel] could say to them, "The entire world belongs to the Holy One, Blessed Be He, He created it and gave [it] to whomever . . . was right in his eyes. Of His own will He gave it to them and of His own will He took it from them and gave it to us."

The reason the Bible begins with the narrative of Creation is to justify the legitimacy of Israel's claim to the land of Canaan. The Lord of Creation can allocate the lands of the earth according to His preferences.

For Maimonides, the opposite tendency prevails. Maimonides doesn't allow the Creation narrative to become absorbed and defined by the narrative of revelation. Each narrative has its own distinct emphasis. On the one hand, the Creation narrative provides a universal path to the love of God. "When a man reflects on these things, studies all these created beings, from the angels and spheres down to human beings and so on, and realizes the Divine Wisdom manifested in them all, his love for God will increase, his soul will thirst, his very flesh will yearn to love God ("Laws of the Foundations of the Torah" 4:12). On the other hand, the revealed law serves a social and political function in building a healthy Jewish community. The knowledge of what is permitted and forbidden "gives primarily composure to the mind. [This is] the precious boon bestowed by God, to promote social well being on earth" (4:13).

> The Law as a whole aims at two things: the welfare of the soul and the welfare of the body. As for the welfare of the soul, it consists in the multitude's acquiring correct opinions. . . . As for the welfare of the body, it comes about by the improvement of their ways of

living one with another. This is achieved through two things. One of them is the abolition of their wronging each other. This is tantamount to every individual among the people not being permitted to act according to his will and up to the limits of his power, but being forced to do that which is useful to the whole. The second thing consists in the acquisition by every human individual of moral qualities that are useful for life in society so that the affairs of the city may be ordered. . . . The Law of *Moses, our Master* has come to bring us both perfections, I mean the welfare of the states of people in their relations with one another through the abolition of reciprocal wrongdoing and through the acquisition of a noble and excellent character. In this way the preservation of the population of the country and their permanent existence in the same order become possible, so that every one of them achieves his first perfection; I mean also the soundness of the beliefs and the giving of correct opinions through which ultimate perfection is achieved. (*Guide* 3:27)

These two narratives, the universal (Creation) and the particular (revelation), are the grounds for two distinct forms of solidarity. Identification with the covenantal community of Israel, its history and its Torah way of life, is the way Jews experienced intimacy with God. This intimacy was often understood in the tradition to mean that God has such a relationship only with Israel. "The Israelite people shall keep the sabbath, observing the sabbath throughout the ages as a covenant for all time: it shall be a sign for all time between Me and the people of Israel" (Exod. 31:16). " 'Between Me and the people of Israel.' But not between Me and the nations of the world" (*Mekhilta*, tractate Shabbata, 2).

R. Akiba says: I shall speak of the prophecies and the praises of Him by whose word the world came into being, before all the nations of the world. For all the nations of the world ask Israel, saying: "What is thy beloved more than another beloved, that thou dost so adjure us" (*Song of Songs* 5:9), that you are so ready to die for Him, and so ready to let yourselves be killed for Him?— For it is said: "Therefore do the maidens love Thee" (ibid. 1:3), meaning, they love Thee unto death. And it is also written: "Nay but for Thy sake are we killed all the day" (Ps. 44:23).—"You are handsome, you are mighty, come and intermingle with us." But the Israelites say to the nations of the world: "Do you know Him? Let us but tell you some of His praise: 'My beloved is white and ruddy,'" etc. (*Song of Songs* 5:10). As soon as the nations of the world hear some of His praise, they say to the Israelites: "We will join you," as it is said: "Whither is thy beloved gone, O thou fairest among women? Whither hath thy beloved turned him, that we may seek him with thee" (ibid. 6:1). The Israelites, however, say to the nations of the world: "You can have no share in Him, but 'My beloved is mine and I am his' (*Song of Songs* 2:16), 'I am my beloved's and my beloved is mine,'" etc. (ibid. 6:3). (*Mekhilta*, tractate Shirata, 3)

For Maimonides, the narrative of the Sinai covenant and the Torah must be read in light of the narrative of the universal God of Creation. As I have shown, the Song of Songs, which was understood in the tradition as describing the exclusive love between Israel and God, was extended by Maimonides to include all philosophical lovers of God regardless of religious or ethnic background.

There is always a danger that the language of intimacy that conveys the experience of God's passionate love for Israel can create a narcissistic frame of mind in which the reality of God revolves exclusively around *my* people's history, *my* rituals and *my* traditions. The passionate attitude that characterizes covenantal communal religious intimacy can overshadow the religious importance of the universal spirit of Creation.

Maimonides used the universal story of Creation to expand the range of halakhic moral and legal responsibility. This is expressed in his explanation of the halakhah prohibiting unfairly harsh treatment of slaves.

> It is forbidden to work any Hebrew slave with rigor. What constitutes work with rigor? It is work which has no fixed limits and unnecessary work which is done only with the purpose of keeping the slave occupied.
>
> Hence the Sages say that the master should not tell his Hebrew slave, "Hoe under the vines until I arrive," because he does not give him a time limit; rather should he say to him, "Hoe until such-and-such a time or up to such-and-such a place."
>
> Thus also one should not say to the Hebrew slave, "Dig up this place," where he has no need for it; nor should he command him even to warm or cool a glass of water for him if he does not need it. If he does so he transgresses a negative commandment, as it is said: "Thou shalt not rule over him with rigor" (Lev. 25:46). Hence the Hebrew slave does for his master only work that has fixed limits and for which there is a need. ("Laws of Slaves" 1:6)

After this moving psychological insight into the meaning of exploitation, it is surprising to read that from a strictly legal perspective, this divinely revealed law applies exclusively to Hebrew slaves.

> It is permitted to work a heathen slave with rigor. Though such is the rule, it is the quality of piety and the way of wisdom that a man be merciful and pursue justice and not make his yoke heavy upon the slave or distress him, but give him to eat and to drink of all foods and drinks.
>
> The Sages of old were wont to let the slave partake of every dish that they themselves ate of and to give the meal of the cattle and of the slaves precedence over their own.... Thus also the master should not disgrace them by hand or by word.... Nor should he heap upon the slave oral abuse and anger, but should rather

speak to him softly and listen to his claims. So it is also explained
in the good paths of Job, in which he prided himself:

    "If I did despise the cause of my manservant,

    Or of my maidservant, when they contended with me. . . .

    Did not He that made me in the womb make him?

    And did not One fashion us in the womb?" (Job 31:13, 15)

("Laws of Slaves" 9:8)

Legally, Torah law prohibits treating a slave with rigor only
in the case of a fellow Jew. The legal constraints that result
from focusing exclusively on the revelation of the Torah to
Israel, for whom communal solidarity defines legal obligation, obligate the family and those who participate in it to
refrain from offensive treatment toward one another. But,
argues Maimonides, when we move beyond Sinai to the God
of Job—the God of Creation: "Did not He that made me
in the womb make Him? And did not One fashion us in
the womb?"—our obligations are expanded to include those
who are not members of the Jewish community.

    Maimonides thus reveals how the theme of Creation
affects the application of the Sinaitic revelation. If we understood and applied the mitzvoth in keeping with the universalistic spirit of Creation, we would realize that the true
intent of God's revelation is to create a people who would
embrace and feel responsible for and compassionate toward
all human beings: "The Israelites, upon whom the Holy
One, blessed be He, bestowed the favor of the Law and laid
upon them statutes and judgments, are [a] merciful people
who have mercy upon all" ("Laws of Slaves" 9:8).

    Just as the narrative of shared suffering in Egypt is a
necessary condition for entrance into the covenant at Sinai
(Passover precedes Shavuot) so the Creation narrative—sol-

idarity with all human beings—is necessary for realizing the true spirit of Torah law. In this way we can understand why the Bible begins with Creation and not with the revealed mitzvoth. Those who wish to follow in the spirit of Maimonides' codification of the laws regarding the treatment of slaves should correct the moral distortions that result from taking the Sinai legal narrative as a justification for discriminating between the moral claims and rights of Jews and non-Jews. Maimonides' statement in the "Laws of Slaves" should be understood to mean that loyalty to the Jewish tradition need not be at the expense of solidarity with all of humanity. The moral weight we give to the Creation story for our understanding of revelation can free us from the either/or dilemma of choosing between particularism and universalism that has paralyzed Jews and distorted the meaning of Judaism throughout modern history. Understanding that the Judaic tradition gave us both the Creation and the Sinai narratives can ameliorate the growing divisions and animosities between secular and religious groups in Israeli society.

In arguing for the contemporary significance of the Maimonidean legacy, I cannot ignore a central theme of Maimonides' philosophy that at first appears irrelevant and alien to modern religious sensibilities. As I showed previously, Maimonides characterized a person who attributed corporeality to God as a heretic. Much of Maimonides' thought was devoted to his relentless struggle against any compromise with anthropomorphic conceptions of God. This concern is foreign to what we now find religiously moving in the biblical narrative. As the biblical scholar Yohanan Muffs has so brilliantly shown, biblical descriptions of God are compelling when understood as a psychological drama involving God as its main "human" protagonist. It is precisely the humanity of God that appeals to Muffs. God becomes more compelling to modern readers of the Bible the more this aspect is emphasized. Muffs cites Saul Lieberman's remark that the most tragic figure in the Bible is God, writing that we are drawn to a God who is part of a human drama and subject to the same emotions, conflicts, and vulnerability that characterize the human condition.

> God appeared before man as a personality: exalted yet fallible and warm. He entered into a contractual relationship with man, became involved in the human condition, experienced exasperation over the hardness of men's hearts, regretting that He had ever created man, was moved by the intercession of Moses and other prophets, broke out into fits of rage over the sinfulness of His people, and was so involved with Israel that despite their sinfulness He actually re-espoused them after having delivered them the bill of divorcement. God appears to experience all the human emotions: love, anger, involvement, indignation, regret, sadness, etc. By so doing, He gives the seal of divinity to the very essence of our humanity. He implicitly says to man: "You cannot know what is above and what is below, but you can know what is in your hearts and in the world. These feelings and reactions and emotions which make up human existence, if illumined by faith and rationality, are all the divinity you can hope for. To be humane is to be divine: as I am holy, so you shall be holy; as I am merciful, so you shall be merciful." Thus, there is only one kind of knowledge that is open to man, the knowledge of God's humanity. ("God and the World: A Jewish View," in *Personhood of God*)

In spite of the demythologization of nature, the modern religious sensibility appears to be moving toward a new remythologization of religious language. Maimonides' preoccupation with idolatry and God's radical otherness and transcendence seems far removed from Muffs's compelling description of God's "humanity." Like Abraham Joshua Heschel, Muffs helps us overcome the embarrassment of talking about God in impassioned human terms. We have discovered the intellectual excitement of capturing the literal sense of biblical anthropomorphic language—the very opposite of the Maimonidean intellectual legacy. The concern with corporeality is not the be all and end all of our commitment to the God of Israel. Maimonides' revulsion against ascribing human moral emotions to God does not horrify us as much as it reminds us of how deeply influenced he was by the Greek conception of perfection as the eternal and unchanging. How do we make sense today of Maimonides' rejection of idolatry? What meaning can we give to the unity-corporeality issue, which appears no longer significant?

In fact, the whole concern with idolatry no longer appears important. The modern spirit of tolerance and the celebration of cultural diversity suggest that the issue of idolatry is not only irrelevant but perhaps also dangerous. If, as Maimonides claimed, the central mission of the election of Israel is to bear witness to the unity of God and to struggle against forms of worship and theological conceptions that undermine the belief in God's unity, we cannot avoid asking today: "What modern expression of idolatry would be incompatible with our affirmation and faith in the unity of God? What are the possible characteristics of modern idolatry that we are called upon to reject?"

In the medieval world, idolatry centered on the object of worship, on what was considered unworthy of worship. I present here an alternative approach to idolatry that is inspired by the talmudic tradition, where not only mistaken objects of worship determine idolatry but also the moral behavior and character of the worshiper.

> How were the Ten Commandments arranged? Five on the one tablet and five on the other. On the one tablet was written: "I am the Lord thy God." And opposite it on the other tablet was written: "You shall not murder." This tells that if one sheds blood, it is accounted to him as though he diminished the divine image. To give a parable. A king of flesh and blood entered a province and the people set up portraits of him, made images of him, and struck coins in his honor. Later on they upset his portraits, broke his images and defaced his coins, thus diminishing the likenesses of the king. So also if one sheds blood it is accounted to him as though he had diminished the divine image. For it is said: "Whoever sheds the blood of man. . . . For in His image Did God make man" (Gen 9:6). (*Mekhilta,* tractate Ba-Hodesh, 7)

The *Mekhilta* identifies the commandment "I am the Lord your God" with "You shall not murder." In destroying a human life and violating the sacredness of a human being, one undermines the presence of God in the world. Faith in God entails an awareness of and respect for the sanctity of human life. When we lose that awareness we can become insensitive to the pain of others; ultimately this can lead to the violent destruction of human life. When we become insensitive to the sanctity of human beings, we are in danger of diminishing God's reality.

In rabbinic literature, the singular, unique worth of every human being derived from the story of Creation. "Beloved and precious are human beings created in the image of God" (Pirkei Avot 3:18). The theme of Creation was also the ground of the Noahide commandment prohibiting murder: "Whoever sheds the blood of man, By man shall his blood be shed; For in His image Did God make man" (Gen 9:6). In the spirit of Maimonides' understanding of the relationship between the themes of Creation and faith in the unity of God, I suggest that any religious vision that ignores the dehumanization of the stranger or of members of other faiths is similar to the sin of idolatry insofar as it can lead to a diminishment of God's reality in the world. Rejecting religious views that differentiate between the human worth of members of one faith and those of another would be a modern application of the talmudic principle "One who rejects idolatry is as one who acknowledges the entire Torah." Shifting the focus of idolatry from mistaken conceptions of God and inappropriate forms of worship to how faith influences our perception of and behavior toward other human beings is a legitimate interpretation and extension of the *Mekhilta*'s juxtaposition of "You shall not murder" with "I am the Lord your God."

Maimonides taught that belief in the unity of the cosmic God of Creation could not be reconciled with a corporeal conception of God. In the spirit of the *Mekhilta* we can claim that belief in God is incompatible with discriminatory practices and negative descriptions of other faiths that are found in many religious traditions, including Judaism. Belief in the unity of God commits us to affirm unambiguously that "one who saves a single human life is as if one saved a whole human world" (T.B. Sanhedrin 4:5). Halakhic scholars and theologians must examine Judaism critically in order to make sure that nothing in the tradition can legitimize the dehumanization of others or weaken belief in the sacredness of every human being created in the image of God.

We cannot denounce triumphalism and dehumanization in other religions or ideologies while ignoring them in our own tradition. As Maimonides argued, we cannot reject paganism among gentiles while excusing it within the Jewish tradition. If we honestly believe that "One who sheds the blood of a human being thereby diminishes the reality of God in the world," we must be careful not to adopt double standards in judging the religious beliefs and moral behavior of others against our own.

The rabbinic tradition took the insight of the *Mekhilta* a step further by using the language of idolatry to describe moral character. "Rabbi Johanan said in the name of R. Simeon b. Shimon b. Yohai: 'Every man in whom is haughtiness of spirit is as though he worshipped idols.' . . . R. Johanan himself said: 'He is as though he had denied the existence of God' " (T.B. Sotah 4b). With regard to the biblical verse "So the people remained at a distance, while Moses approached the thick cloud where God was" (Exod. 20:18), the midrash asks what enabled Moses to approach the "thick cloud":

> "But Moses Drew Near unto the Thick Darkness." What brought him this distinction? His meekness. For it is said: "Now the man Moses was very meek" (ibid., 12:3). Scripture tells that whosoever is meek will cause the Shekinah to dwell with man on earth, as it is said: "For thus saith the High and Lofty One that inhabiteth eternity, whose name is Holy: I dwell in the high and holy place, with him also that is of a contrite and humble spirit" (Isa. 57:15). . . . But whosoever is proud of heart causes the land to be defiled and the Shekinah to withdraw, as it is said: "Whoso is haughty of eye and proud of heart, him will I not suffer" (ibid., 101:5). Furthermore, one who is proud of heart is designated an abomination, as it is said: "Everyone that is proud in heart is an abomination of the Lord" (Prov. 16:5). Idols are also designated an abomina-

tion, as it is said: "And thou shalt not bring an abomination into thy house" (Deut. 7:26). Hence, just as idolatry defiles the land and causes the Shekinah to withdraw, so he who is proud of heart causes the earth to become defiled and the Shekinah to withdraw. (*Mekhilta,* tractate Ba-Hodesh, 9)

These rabbinic texts direct attention away from metaphysical truth-claims about God to the human characteristics necessary for living in His presence. These texts are not the teachings of secular humanists but of pious rabbinic teachers that explain the moral implications of the life of faith.

Many theologians would disagree with my placing the focus of idolatry and the meaning of faith on moral behavior and on the affirmation of the sanctity of human life. They regard the story of the binding of Isaac as the essence of genuine faith, in which obedience to God transcends human knowledge and morality. Yeshayahu Leibowitz, one of the most significant theologians in modern Israel, characterized the ʿaqedah (the binding of Isaac) as the most eloquent and appropriate symbol of Judaism. He contrasted Judaism, in which Abraham was called upon to sacrifice his child in the service of God, with Christianity, in which God the Father sacrificed His son for the sake of humanity. For Leibowitz, giving precedence to ethics (the Creation narrative) over complete, uncritical obedience to the mitzvoth (the Sinai narrative) contradicts Judaism's understanding of the life of worship and borders on an idolatrous humanism in which man rather than God is at the center of the universe.

As I argued in *A Living Covenant* and in *A Heart of Many Rooms,* I regard neither of Leibowitz's images of religion as sacrifice—of humanity for God or of God for humanity—as compelling because I prefer an understanding of the covenantal relationship between God and Israel in which the fullness of the human person is affirmed. In contrast to choosing the 'aqedah as the paradigm of faith in God, I choose the story of Abraham arguing with God for the people of Sodom in which God is expected to act in accordance with Abraham's understanding of justice and morality. "Far be it from You to do such a thing, to bring death upon the innocent as well as the guilty, so that innocent and guilty fare alike. Far be it from You! Shall not the Judge of all the earth deal justly?" (Gen. 18:25). Abraham continues to argue by appealing first for fifty, then forty-five, forty, and so on, righteous men as just cause to spare Sodom. The model of Abraham's pleading on behalf of Sodom suggests that God accepts the legitimacy of Abraham's moral arguments. If this were not so, God would have silenced his protestations immediately with a "My ways are not your ways" response. Or He could have short-circuited the discussion by telling Abraham at the very beginning that there were not even ten righteous people in Sodom. Instead God allows Abraham's tenacious and lengthy plea on behalf of Sodom. It is as if He were celebrating Abraham's protest and inviting him to persist in bringing his moral intuitions to judgment of His actions.

Just as Abraham does not doubt his own moral sense of justice in arguing with God so we in the modern world must not sacrifice our moral intuitions on the alter of loyalty to our particular religious traditions. We must not be intimidated by a "My ways are not your ways" argument when we feel critical of the moral teachings of our tradition.

I believe that God's confirmation of Abraham's understanding of justice is analogous to Maimonides' encouragement to people not to repress their intellectual curiosity and sense of honesty but to accept knowledge and truth whatever the source. Maimonides was prepared to reinterpret the entire biblical tradition had Aristotle demonstrated the truth of the doctrine of the eternity of the universe. The analogy between Maimonides' willingness to reinterpret his tradition on the basis of Aristotelian philosophical demonstration and the legitimacy of our reinterpretation of the Jewish tradition in light of our moral knowledge is an important one.

Many students of Maimonides would disagree with this argument, pointing to the epistemic difference between moral knowledge and theoretical truth. For Maimonides, moral claims had only the certainty of "accepted opinion" and lacked the logical weight of demonstrative truths. Because our moral claims do not have the logical status of demonstrative truths, we cannot use Maimonides' willingness to reinterpret the Bible to justify the use of morality to reinterpret the Jewish tradition. Nevertheless, I would argue that many of our moral beliefs that are universally acknowledged by people of goodwill, such as not inflicting undeserved suffering on another, respecting the sacredness of all human life, and not arbitrarily discriminating between persons in the administration of justice, are as intellectually and humanly compelling to us as Aristotelian demonstrative truths were to Maimonides. For Maimonides, nothing was sacrosanct if it entailed a conflict with truth. We today must not suppress our deepest moral intuitions when evaluating the moral and legal claims of our tradition. Love of God as mediated by our particular traditions must always remain a critical love because God's acceptance of our humanity—

which is the basis of our covenant with God—includes our understanding of justice.

My claim that there are precedents within Maimonides and the talmudic tradition for bringing a universal, moral perspective to the application of traditional Halakhah should not be understood as an assertion that this is what Maimonides and the rabbinic tradition intended. I am aware that the talmudic tradition did not fully exploit the moral and legal possibilities of such statements as "Beloved are human beings created in the image of God" and "One who saves a single human life is as if one saved a whole human world." Similarly, Maimonides did not universally apply the theme of Creation found in his "Laws of Slaves" to all the halakhic laws that differentiate between the rights of Jews and non-Jews. There is no doubt that Maimonides' philosophy was more concerned with correcting mistaken conceptions of God than with correcting morally problematic halakhoth.

In reinterpreting the implications of Maimonidean and rabbinic texts for understanding modern idolatry or for correcting discriminatory halakhic legislation, I do not claim that I follow the intentions of either the Talmud or Maimonides. But neither Maimonides nor rabbinic teachers have control over the implications or applications of their rich and suggestive teachings. I have argued that there are resources within the tradition for its own self-correction. The Creation narrative has a power and life of its own independent of how it was applied in the biblical and rabbinic traditions. The scope of its ethical and legal implications is not restricted to how it was used in the past.

The argument for placing the Jewish particularistic narrative within a universalistic framework should not be misunderstood to mean that particularity and symbolic ritual must be abolished and replaced by universal moral content. The justification for most of the commandments need not be based solely on moral reasons. The election of Israel can be understood as God's validation of particularity. Human dignity and cultural identities grow out of particular histories, stories, memories, and ways of life. Election, therefore, can signify the legitimacy of a particular people or community who are building a spiritual way of life through the narrative of their own history and traditions.

In other words, Sinai and revelation can be appreciated without claiming that election makes sense only in terms of a universal redemptive mission. Nineteenth- and twentieth-century German Jewish philosophers traumatized by Spinoza's and Kant's critiques of Judaism, which identified Jewish law and peoplehood with tribalism rather than universal morality and rationality, legitimated the Jewish experience by interpreting it in universalistic terms. In contrast, I argue that justifying our national existence by claiming that we are the instruments for realizing God's messianic redemptive plan is both unnecessary and morally and politically dangerous (for example, it would rule out territorial compromises even when Israel's national security is not placed in jeopardy).

Our coming home, our ceasing to be a wandering, vulnerable people, and our quest for normalcy are intrinsically legitimate without the claim that the rebirth of Israel is essential to God's redemption of humanity. Whether our national renaissance benefits humanity as a whole should be left for other nations to decide. Our attention should be focused on the religious and moral vitality of our own society. Must our feelings of solidarity with all Jewish people and our commitment to Jewish nationalism inevitably lead to our ignoring the rights and dignity of minorities and strangers in our midst? If there is any positive meaning to the mission of the Jews and to their election it is in showing how the universal theme of Creation can correct the vitality of the particular without destroying it.

There are Jews who believe that emphasizing solidarity with all of humanity will drain the vitality from Jewish particularity. They therefore emphasize the particular above the universal, the rituals of Sabbath observance and tefillin as unique expressions of Judaism. Many Orthodox observant Jews in Israel and in the diaspora as well as the rabbinic establishment in Israel respond vociferously to public communal violations of ritual halakhic practice while relinquishing concern for the ethical and moral quality of our society to secular and Reform Jews. It is disturbing to see Jews who worry about public *kashrut* and Sabbath observance but don't seem to be bothered by the unjust treatment or exploitation of foreign workers and minorities. This mistaken, tragic dichotomy distorts the unity of the Sinai and Creation narratives.

We can make claims about the religious significance of the rebirth of Israel from two perspectives: a messianic and a normative one. The Exodus as a model for understanding God's actions in history points to a history of salvation and redemption. When understood within an Exodus-messianic framework, the rebirth of the state of Israel is referred to—as it is in the official prayer for the state's welfare—as "the beginning of our redemption." Rabbi Kook justified the religious community's participation in the secular Zionist revolution in messianic terms. For Rabbi Kook, the people of Israel as God's elect are the instruments of salvation in history. For those influenced by Rabbi Kook's teachings, giving up a messianic understanding of Israel negates the religious significance and purpose of the Jewish people in history and of our modern national renaissance.

However, this is not our only religious option. As Maimonides taught us, the Sinai moment can also serve as an orienting framework from which to understand the meaning of Judaism. Talmudic Judaism's concern with study and mitzvoth, with living a disciplined life and serving God in every aspect of daily life, redirected religious passion from the external arena of history to the internal domain of character, and individual and communal behavior. The elaborate development of Halakhah in the rabbinic tradition enabled us to move away from an exclusive concern with a history of salvation. The religious ideal of talmudic Judaism lay not in the yearning for salvation and anticipation of the Messiah but in seeking to infuse the mundane and routine situations of daily life with a sense of God's presence. Halakhah leads us to acknowledge God's kingdom in history (*qabalat malkhut shamayim*) by acknowledging the authority of divine commandments in our daily life (*qabalat mitzvot*).

The all-inclusive, single-minded pursuit of God implicit in "In all your ways, know Him" and "Let all your deeds be for the sake of heaven"—rather than messianism—fueled Maimonides' religious passion (see the *Eight Chapters* 5, "Laws Concerning Character Traits" 3:2–3, and *Guide* 3:51). The movement away from an event-based theology found in the Talmud and in Maimonides can provide us with a different perspective on the religious significance of the rebirth of Israel. Today we have an opportunity to reestablish the normative moment of Sinai, rather than the Exodus story, as the primary framework for evaluating the significance of Jewish history. To be religiously significant, a historical event does not have to be situated between the moment of the Exodus and the coming of the Messiah. It can be significant by encouraging us to discover new depths in the foundational moment of Israel's election as a covenantal people.

I respond religiously to the establishment of the state of Israel from a Sinai-covenantal model for the following reasons. In reestablishing the Jewish nation in its ancient homeland, Jews have taken responsibility for all aspects of social life. The divine call to become a holy nation committed to implementing the letter and spirit of the Torah must influence our economic, political, and religious institutions. Through the establishment of the state of Israel, we are called upon to demonstrate the moral and spiritual power of the Torah to respond to the challenges of daily life. Our record of success is far from evident. But even failure does not diminish the religious significance of Israel insofar as it can teach us about who we are and how far we are from the self-congratulatory descriptions of ourselves as the children of the prophets and God's elect.

I am grateful to God and offer prayers of thanksgiving and praise for living in a time when the Jewish people have such enormous religious and moral opportunities. I disagree with the claim that Zionism and the rebirth of the state of Israel must necessarily lead to the reghettoization and tribalization of the Jewish people. I also disagree with the Haredi Orthodox repudiation of modernity and its claim that only an insulated form of Judaism can guarantee the future of Israel as a Jewish society.

Israel is not a return to a religious or political ghetto where Jewish particularity and universality conflict, where symbolic religious ritual and the passion for social justice are unrelated expressions of loyalty to traditional Judaism. Israel represents the birth of a healthy society that seeks to create a nation like all other nations. The demythologization of the Jewish people is one of the great gifts of Israeli society to the Jewish people. Statehood has shattered the credibility of the grandiose sermons about the nature of the Jewish people that rabbis often give in the diaspora. Although it is true that history reveals our heroic determination not to be defeated by the enemies of Judaism, and although the mystery of our survival in history evokes admiration and wonder, the truth is that we are also *nebuch* a people. (I don't quite know how to translate *nebuch*. It is a technical term.) We are people with many flaws, but we are also a very decent people. Pettiness and cruelty as well as acts of compassion and concern for the well-being of others can be found in our society. This is what it means to discover that we are *nebuch* a people. In the 1930s there were Jews who thought, "Isn't it wonderful that we can now have Jewish prostitutes and thieves as a sign of our normalcy?" Today we are no longer proud of how very normal we have become.

Yet by allowing our bodies, not just our heads, to be visible, our ideal of normalcy has restored dignity to Jews and the freedom to engage in every human activity. As I noted earlier, the Jewish body was sacrificed to the Jewish mind for more than two thousand years. I will never forget my first visit to a religious kibbutz, where I met a kibbutznik who was anxious to show me his home. I was sure he was going to show me his library or his rare books because these were the things I thought religious Jews took pride in. Instead, he showed me a tree he had planted. "What a transformation of consciousness," I thought. Not his books but his tree, the work of his hands. For me this was truly a sign of the success of the Zionist quest for normalcy. Not the return of prophecy as Rabbi Kook anticipated but the legitimization of feeling free and able to engage in the fullness and diversity of human creativity, intellectual or physical.

I have thus far suggested how we can provide a religious response to the rebirth of nationhood without placing our national renaissance within the continuum of a redemptive messianic process. Religious Zionists influenced by the dramatic victory of the Six-Day War need not believe that territorial compromise entails the loss of the vitality and the energizing power of our national renaissance.

There is, however, another, equally important issue affecting a large segment of Israeli society. Many secular Israelis now realize the great mistake they made in relinquishing their spiritual heritage to the Orthodox practitioners of Judaism and the official rabbinic establishment. Israeli educators yearn to discover the significance of their heritage. On one level, they are proud of the secular achievements of the state and are committed to the cultural and intellectual traditions of liberal democratic societies. But at the same time, they wish to retrieve the vitality of their own Jewish heritage. If we fail to help these Israelis become intellectually adequate to reconnect with their tradition, we will further aggravate the religious-secular polarization that poisons the political climate of Israeli society, threatening its future stability. In responding to this issue I offer an approach to traditional Judaism that is less authoritarian and intimidating and more supportive of Israelis who wish to integrate the Jewish tradition with modernity.

Many in the religious Zionist community are positively disposed toward secular Israelis because of the secular community's commitment to the continuity of the Jewish people and because the state of Israel serves as a powerful countervailing force against assimilation. We should not make the mistake of setting peoplehood against covenantal consciousness as two irreconcilable focuses of Jewish identity. The "Who is a Jew?" debate is less a matter of religion versus peoplehood than it is one of how to define the nature of this people. The concepts of family and shared national destiny are indispensable to an explanation of the meaning of Judaism. The biblical narrative that defined the Jewish people's self-understanding unabashedly combined the themes of the national liberation from Egypt (shared destiny), the Sinai revelation (shared covenantal consciousness), and the prophetic interpretation of Jewish history (election and redemption). The separation of this unified conception into distinct and conflicting elements occurred only in the modern world.

Nonetheless, traditional Jews who make Sinai the guiding metaphor of their cultural-religious lives cannot ignore the strong national and communal notions that underlie the Jewish heritage. The theologian who hopes to make sense of Judaism cannot focus exclusively on religious doctrine, halakhic practice, and sacred texts but must also explain the centrality of the people of Israel, which "even if it sins, remains Israel." Communal solidarity is a vital characteristic of Jewish spirituality.

As the state of Israel developed, so did the Jewish community's sense of memory and connection to Jewish history, which had been eroded by twentieth-century individualism and secularism. This powerful restoration of memory, of not only living with the needs of the present but also carrying the weight of the past, is fundamental to Jewish identity. The existence of Israel has created conditions that make the rehabilitation of historical memory a living experience for contemporary Jewry. It is no wonder that Israel is the focus and energizing power of Jewish peoplehood today.

Israel is also a major catalyst for reopening involvement with the Jewish tradition. I do not claim that most Israelis are seeking spiritual meaning in their lives but only that Israel has created a national framework that keeps alive Jewish peoplehood and the will to continue the story of Jewish history. In establishing the state within the biblical homeland, secular Zionists made a decision against assimilation and against breaking their ties with Jewish history. The fact that a community exists in which people consciously affirm their connection with Jewish history is a necessary, albeit insufficient, condition for reviving connection with the tradition and its spiritual concerns.

In spite of their rejection of many of the values and institutions which traditional Jews regard as sacred and their radically secular interpretation of Jewish history, secular Israelis continue to participate in the body politic of the Jewish people. They have revived the sacred Hebrew language into a living language of everyday life and literature, and they share many of the traditional texts, symbols, and festivals that are essential features of the Jewish tradition.

We must never forget that secular Israelis perceive themselves as members of the family of the Jewish people. Their sense of community is not based on a shared faith but on the social bond between people who share a common home and memories. Families may be divided over the nature of their goals, yet when they live together and benefit from the same social, economic, and welfare institutions, they share a common concern for the continuity and vitality of that family.

The continuity of the Jewish people as a distinct historical entity was a particular concern of the twentieth-century Orthodox leader and theologian Rabbi Joseph B. Soloveitchik, who devoted his life to restoring and deepening the spiritual dimension of Jewish consciousness. Rabbi Soloveitchik believed that because Israel made Jews self-conscious and visible and thus counteracted the assimilationist tendencies of American Jewry, it had covenantal significance. He was therefore prepared to embrace the Zionist enterprise despite its ideological opposition to the basic tenets of his religious thought. He understood and appreciated the significance of Israel as a means of reviving Jewish identity and solidarity after the Holocaust and in the face of powerful forces of assimilation in American life. In *Kol Dodi Dofeq* (It is the voice of my beloved that knocketh), Rabbi Soloveitchik introduced the bold theological category of *berit goral*, the covenant of shared destiny, which, he claimed, was a necessary condition for participating in *berit ye'ud*, the covenant of shared religious aspiration.

Rabbi Soloveitchik's approach differs from other religious responses to Zionism, which use the language of a theology of history to integrate secular Zionism into their religious worldviews. Rabbi Kook's dialectical, mystical theology of history absorbed the seemingly heretical revolution of Zionism into a grand scheme that transformed it into an energizing agent capable of releasing latent spiritual powers within the Jewish people. He understood secularization as a necessary stage in the process leading to the final vindication and revitalization of Judaism. It was a preparatory stage that would be followed by a renewed outburst of spiritual and prophetic energies within the Jewish people. Rabbi Soloveitchik's approach makes no reference to metaphysics or historical dialectics but rests on straightforward factual and empirical claims. After experiencing the trauma of the Holocaust and witnessing the danger of assimilation of the American Jewish community, Rabbi Soloveitchik was impressed by the fact that Israel was a powerful and effective force in strengthening Jewish identity.

The opponents of the views of Rabbis Soloveitchik and Kook in the Orthodox camp perceive only danger in the secularizing tendencies of Israeli society. They refuse to ascribe religious significance to the rebirth of the state of Israel and view Israeli secular culture as a threat to the future of Judaism. This becomes painfully evident on Israel's Independence Day, when many religious Jews offer prayers of thanksgiving to God (Hallel) for their having returned home after two thousand years of exile and greet one another with the traditional *hag sameach* (joyful holiday), whereas most Haredi Jews go about their affairs as if nothing of religious significance had happened on this day. Rabbis Soloveitchik and Kook, on the other hand, believe in the inevitable failure of secularism among the Jewish people. This belief underlies Rabbi Soloveitchik's explanation of Maimonides' linking of messianic redemption with Israel's *teshuvah* (repentance). "All the prophets charged the people concerning repentance. Only through repentance will Israel be redeemed, and the Torah already offered the assurance that Israel will, in the closing period of this exile, finally repent, and thereupon be immediately redeemed" ("Laws of Repentance" 7:5).

Maimonides accepts the talmudic view that *ge'ulah*, redemption, is dependent upon teshuvah, which seems to imply that redemption is not inevitable. Belief in a *possible* redemption would undermine the central religious conviction regarding the certainty and necessity of the coming of the Messiah. Rabbi Soloveitchik makes the ingenious exegetical move of interpreting Maimonides' position as a statement of belief in Israel's eventual teshuvah. Rather than base his certainty in redemption on divine grace, Rabbi Soloveitchik invokes a quasi-mystical belief in the Jewish psyche, which, he believes, has been programmed by God to choose the path of teshuvah sooner or later.

> But if one accepts Maimonides' opinion and sides with Rabbi Eliezer, who says that the coming of the Messiah is dependent upon repentance and that if it does not take place then there will be no redemption; how is it possible to declare, "I believe with complete faith in the advent of the Messiah and though he may tarry I will await his coming every day"; it is possible that he will tarry indefinitely if Israel does not repent; what sense is there in awaiting his coming daily?
>
> Maimonides was not oblivious to this contradiction and he went on to say: "The Torah has already assured us that Israel will finally repent at the end of their exile and immediately be redeemed." Though this is not an unconditional promise regard-

ing the advent of the Messiah there is an assurance that *Knesset Israel* as an entity will not be extinguished and will never be exterminated. This promise has dual significance: *Knesset Israel* will never be wiped out physically and will never terminate its existence through spiritual assimilation or contamination. True, there are countless numbers of Jews who have wandered afar and gone astray in alien pastures—but "in the end Israel will repent." It emerges from this that *faith in the coming of the Messiah is dependent upon our faith in Knesset Israel.* This implies that however far the Jewish people may go astray and become alienated from Judaism and fall prey to assimilation, in the end it will be restored! If we allow this faith to waver, then our entire belief in the coming of the Messiah is undermined! (*On Repentance*, pp. 134–35)

Although I fully agree that without a Jewish people there is no Judaism, I differ from both Rabbi Soloveitchik and Rabbi Kook on the certainty of the ultimate spiritual renewal of the Jewish people. Israel has succeeded in helping us become a nation like all nations. The spiritual future of diaspora Jewry, however, is far from secure. In earlier essays I argued passionately for the spiritual renaissance which I believed would necessarily follow in the aftermath of the Six-Day War. Perhaps it was listening to my own sermons that influenced my belief that Israel would become the central organizing force for the spiritual renewal of Judaism.

Today I admit to having serious doubts about this sanguine belief. I now share Yeshayahu Leibowitz's skepticism about the positive influence of Israel on the future of Judaism. I also share his fear that the Jewish people are on the verge of losing their covenantal identity by becoming a secular people with no more than a shallow sentimental attachment to the Torah and to the tradition of a Torah, text-centered community. I am also convinced by those who argue that Israelis have the will to survive as a sovereign political nation without making the Torah and the Jewish tradition important components of their self-understanding. In contrast to Rabbis Kook and Soloveitchik's belief in the inevitability of Jews remaining a Torah people, I fear that the secularization of the Jewish people is a real possibility—and the disappearance of the Jewish people as traditionally understood is equally possible.

I should note here, however, that not all segments of Jewish society acknowledge the problem of modernity. Some do not recognize modernity as a cultural paradigm shift and continue to view the so-called new Jewish community as filling traditional categories. In spite of the indifference of many Jews to the Torah, these people believe that the spark of belief in the Torah is still alive in the Jewish soul. They fail to grasp how far we have moved from the conception of the Jewish people that informed Maimonides' legitimization of coercion in divorce proceedings.

> If a person who may be legally compelled to divorce his wife refuses to do so, an Israelite court in any place and at any time may scourge him until he says "I consent." He may then write a get, and it is a valid get. . . . And why is this get not null and void, seeing that it is the product of duress, whether exerted by heathens or by Israelites? Because duress applies only to him who is compelled and pressed to do something which the Torah does not obligate him to do, for example, one who is lashed until he consents to sell something or give it away as a gift. On the other hand, he whose evil inclination induces him to violate a commandment or commit a transgression, and who is lashed until he does what he is obligated to do, or refrains from what he is forbidden to do, cannot be regarded as a victim of duress; rather, he has brought duress upon himself by submitting to his evil intention. There-

fore this man who refuses to divorce his wife, inasmuch as he desires to be of the Israelites, to abide by all the commandments,
and to keep away from transgressions—it is only his inclination
that has overwhelmed him—once he is lashed until his inclination is weakened and he says "I consent," it is the same as if he
had given the get voluntarily. ("Laws of Divorce," 2:20)

Even though free choice is a necessary condition of valid
legal acts in general and of divorce in particular, Maimonides argued that the implicit assumption of membership in
the Jewish community was sufficient justification for coercion. Under such circumstances coercion could be understood as a form of liberation, an act that freed someone from
the shackles of ignorance or passion which temporarily pre-
vented his doing what he had tacitly agreed to. In calling
himself a Jew, an individual implicitly assumes the values and
obligations of the normative framework of Judaism. Coercion, therefore, should not be viewed as an external imposi-
tion upon one's free will, but rather as a means of liberating
Jews from the psychological pressures and constraints that
prevent them from fulfilling their true desires.

Notwithstanding the problematic nature of Maimonides' argument, the crucial point is that for Maimonides,
membership in the community of Israel presupposed tacit
assent to the authority of Torah and Halakhah. This assumption no longer exists in the modern world because the Jewish
people no longer define themselves as a Torah people. The
disappearance of this assumption is evident in the recurring
preoccupation with the "Who is a Jew?" issue. The question is not only which rabbi has legitimate legal authority
to serve on the "membership committee" that decides who
is eligible to enter the Jewish community but also whether

there are any necessary normative conditions for membership. In other words, are there fundamental beliefs and practices that are constitutive of Jewish identity?

Many Orthodox rabbinic and political leaders continue to speak as if no radical change has taken place since the time of Maimonides. By their public announcements and extreme preoccupation with the Conservative and Reform movements, it is clear that they do not appreciate the extent and seriousness of the alienation of Israelis from their heritage and of the rapid assimilation of diaspora Jewry. They have no hesitation in confronting all Israeli Jews, regardless of beliefs and commitments, in the name of the Torah and the authority of Halakhah as if these were universally acknowledged legal and value frameworks. Because they have not come to terms with the radical break with the founding moments that traditionally constituted Jewish identity, they continue using a discourse that strains the limits of credibility. It is as if we could still legislate compliance with Jewish dietary laws in Israel. The oddity of their religious posture vis-à-vis the secular community is due to their failure to grasp the extent to which Jewish consciousness has changed.

Because of my belief in the serious challenge secularization poses to the continuity of the Jewish tradition and the Jewish people, I recognize the need to interpret Judaism in a way that would empower Israelis and Jews throughout the world to reengage with their tradition. There is value in opening up a discussion on the tradition without making the assumption that Jews are on the road to teshuvah. A discussion concerning the Jewish tradition is open-ended. We do not know beforehand what direction such a discussion will take or how the tradition will speak to the diverse temperaments and sensibilities that exist both in Israel and in the diaspora. Given the deep fragmentation of the Jewish community, we need to be wary of solutions that demand a coherent, monolithic understanding of Judaism. Instead we must recognize that there is a tradition waiting to be addressed and waiting to speak to us. The question is how to speak to and how to listen to that tradition.

One can believe in the importance of seriously engaging the tradition while fully acknowledging the many frameworks that inform Jewish identity and communal life. My underlying assumption is that we live in a time when 1) the Zionist belief in the inevitable secularization of Israel has been questioned; 2) the normative consensus that once claimed the Torah as the single constitutive component of Jewish identity has disappeared; and 3) there is a yearning among secular Israelis to become engaged and connected even minimally with the Jewish tradition. There is a sense of crisis but also a feeling of excitement about the future. The crisis centers on the massive assimilation of diaspora Jewry and the cultural discontinuity and alienation of Israelis from their Jewish past. The excitement is due to the powerful impact of Israel in restoring the vitality of Jewish peoplehood and historical memory and in liberating Jews from the embarrassment of being visible in Western culture.

The crucial issue of our age is not how to revive the authority of Halakhah but how to revive the Jewish discussion. Halakhah and rabbinic authority have meaning when a community shares a common authoritative normative framework. But we live in an age that lacks agreement on such foundational frameworks. Sinai, election, and Moses' vision of Jews as "a nation of priests and a holy people" do not define our daily lives, nor do they cause us sleepless nights.

Our problem is not the different denominational movements of modern Judaism or who has the authority to decide Halakhic issues. The crucial issue is how Jews who are not prepared for a leap of faith and are far removed from a commitment to Halakhah and rabbinic authority can be encouraged to reengage with Jewish traditional texts and feel intellectually empowered to participate in Judaism's ongoing interpretive tradition.

In the past, Jewish thought was often expressed in the form of interpretation. The goal of learning was not to discover the radically new and uncharted but to deepen and expand the discussion of previous generations. Intellectual creativity was nurtured by what one had received. One always returned to Sinai and traditional texts. The innovative student uncovered and expanded the spiritual possibilities of the tradition. It was natural, therefore, for most literary and philosophical works to be presented as commentary. This would explain the spirit of the following midrash: "Scripture, Mishnah, Halachot, Talmud, Toseftot, Haggadot, and even what a faithful disciple would in the future say in the presence of his master, were all communicated to Moses at Sinai" (Leviticus Rabbah, 'Aharei Mot, 22:1). The legacy of the interpretive tradition cannot be reclaimed without a new orientation to the classical texts of our tradition and to the meaning of participation in an interpretive community. As I have shown, we are no longer a text-centered people. The culture of interpretation as an ongoing engagement with what was considered to be the revealed word of God has been broken. I therefore believe that one of the primary tasks of Jewish philosophy today is to provide an approach to the Torah that can retrieve the vitality of the Jewish interpretive tradition.

Presenting Judaism as a closed system with a fixed menu prepared exactly according to divine requirements can stifle and inhibit genuine engagement with the tradition. I therefore make the following distinction in order to counteract this dogmatic and naive understanding of Judaism and, more important, to create an inviting atmosphere, so that even those who are indifferent to revelation and Halakhic practice can participate in and enhance Judaism's interpretive tradition. I shall distinguish between the concepts of Torah and Halakhah, two distinct categories that are often conflated by those who lack an understanding of the rich, multidimensional nature of Judaism as an interpretive culture.

The term *Torah,* in its broadest sense, can best be understood to include both what was considered the revealed word of God and the long history of interpretation. The Torah, therefore, is comprised of the written Torah (biblical literature), and the oral Torah (midrash, talmud), legal and haggadic works, medieval and modern responsa literature, Kabbalah, hasidism, medieval and modern Jewish philosophy, theology, poetry, and literature. The Torah spans generations of different religious sensibilities, offering the broadest possible definition of the scope of Jewish spirituality. Legalism and romanticism, rationalism and mysticism are some of the directions this discussion took in the past. Jewish history and identity have been shaped by the various directions of the discussion and by the variety of questions and problems with which the tradition had to cope.

Just as the possibilities of raising legitimate questions are enormous, so too are the directions and paths a Torah discussion can take. One need not be confined to or constricted by what medieval or modern philosophers defined as the essence of Judaism or by what the religious community considers the authentic interpretive texts of the Jewish tradition.

The language of the Torah is not restricted to a particular moment in the tradition but covers the ongoing interpretation of the Torah throughout history. The mitzvah of *talmud torah,* studying the Torah, is not fulfilled only by studying law in its final, authoritative form. The benediction recited every morning, "Blessed are You Lord our God who has sanctified us with His commandments and commanded us to be engaged in the words of the Torah," is valid even when the texts studied are not considered to be the revealed word of God or do not convey the accepted halakhic practice of the community. The blessing is valid and not considered "uttering God's name in vain" regardless of whether the texts are those of *Beit Shamai* (the Halakhah usually preferred the rival views of *Beit Hillel*) or of later scholars, such as the discussions of twentieth-century teachers of the Torah. In the context of a Torah discussion I am concerned not only with final decisions and accepted practice but with whatever conjectures and ideas have been articulated even tentatively during the course of Jewish intellectual history.

Modern talmudic scholars and Jewish thinkers should uncover the different directions available for the engagement with the biblical and talmudic traditions. It is also important to show how traditional texts can make room for new possibilities. Again, by "traditional texts" I do not mean the authoritative normative tradition of Halakhah but all the elements of the Torah: the legal and the literary, the definitive and the tentative. I am often fascinated by and would like to retrieve the conjectures and suggestions that surfaced in rabbinic discussions in the Talmud even when they did not directly influence authoritative normative practice.

The concept of *Halakhah* differs from this notion of the Torah insofar as it refers to the accepted authoritative body of law that governs and regulates community practice. Halakhah is a legal system—albeit one that relates to areas of life which lie beyond the purview of most secular legal systems—and is conceptually bound up with the notions of power and authority. A complete analysis of Halakhah would require us to examine the philosophical, political, and sociological foundations of legal authority, legal reasoning, and legal decision making.

The force of a halakhic decision is determined by who the judge is, not simply what reasons are given. The right to be listened to is no less important than the cogency of legal argumentation. Many of the struggles between rival groups within the halakhic community in Israel today center on which halakhic authorities have the right to render decisions on the status of women and family law, the borders of the Land of Israel, the peace process and territorial compromise, and so on. Halakhic authorities interpret how the tradition should be applied in present-day situations. Living within the confines of Halakhah presupposes an advanced stage of religious commitment to conform to the weight of authority of the halakhic tradition. An exploration of the Torah, however, does not require or presuppose such a commitment.

There are many individuals who are not satisfied with just an intellectual engagement with the tradition but also seek practical guidance on how to embrace traditional halakhic forms of life. It would be extremely helpful if they were encouraged to view Halakhah as an educational rather than a legal system. This would allow selective experimentation, which need not pass the test of halakhic consistency or receive formal legitimization by traditional rabbinical authorities. Although this may prove threatening to those concerned with protecting the authority, consistency, and intellectual integrity of the halakhic system, it could also be invaluable for the community that seeks ways of reengaging the tradition without severing its roots in the modern world. Viewing Halakhah from an educational, experimental perspective need not threaten the legal integrity of the halakhic system because this orientation neither claims nor requires halakhic legitimization. Encouraging individuals to begin a spiritual process and to select and experiment with halakhic forms should not be confused with modern attempts at creating a new Halakhah. This position should not be identified with legal anarchy but rather with a patient understanding of the difficulties of overcoming the deep estrangement that many Jews feel toward their tradition.

When Halakhah becomes an invitation to listen to and explore traditional forms of Jewish spirituality, it becomes more inviting and inclusive, less authoritarian. Halakhah could be understood less in terms of a legal system with enormous, weighty claims of authority and more as an experimental educational system that suggests rather than dictates the forms of Jewish spiritual living. Halakhah would thus be understood as a more inviting and flexible mode of discourse.

Many Israelis are disturbed and angered by the dangerous polarization between a ghetto vision of Judaism that repudiates modernity and a radical secularism that ridicules the tradition. In relaxing the language of the Jewish tradition, we would empower those who are drawn to the Jewish tradition but who nonetheless feel intimidated or repelled by the traditional authoritarian mode of religious discourse. Inviting Jews to reconnect with the Torah is especially important at this time in Jewish history because the crucial problem for the majority of Jews today is not Halakhah but the lack of identification with and appreciation of their Jewish heritage. Our problem is the tone-deafness of Jews to the music of the Jewish tradition. The problem of our age cannot be resolved by offering halakhic answers but by creating a community that will be interested in asking halakhic questions.

The serious new religious issues facing our generation cannot be resolved by establishing a universally accepted authoritative body to render halakhic decisions, such as a new Sanhedrin. The issue is not a lack of legal authority. New halakhic decisions will not change the direction of Jewish history unless we first rehabilitate the meaning of being a Torah-covenantal community. Halakhah and the rabbinate will change when people concerned with egalitarianism, human rights, and social justice view the Jewish tradition as the natural context in which to express their concerns. This will only come about, however, when we develop a compelling, intellectual, and moral vision of what it means to be an interpretive, text-centered community.

# References

All quotations from Babylonian Talmud (abbreviated as T.B.) are taken from the edition by I. Epstein. London: Soncino Press, 1961–1990.

Ahad Ha'am. "The Sabbath and Zionism" (Hebrew), in *Kol Kitvei Ahad Ha'am*. Jerusalem: Jewish Publishing House, 1956.

Avineri, Shlomo. *The Making of Modern Zionism: The Intellectual Origins of the Jewish State*. London: Weidenfeld and Nicolson, 1981.

Ben Ezer, Ehud, ed. *Unease in Zion*. Quadrangle Books and Jerusalem Academic Press, 1974.

Briggs, C. A., and E. G. Briggs. *A Critical and Exegetical Commentary on the Book of Psalms*. Edinburgh: Clark, 1976.

Greenberg, Moshe. "Three Conceptions of the Torah in Hebrew Scriptures," in Greenberg, *Studies in the Bible and Jewish Thought*. Philadelphia: Jewish Publication Society, 1995.

Halbertal, Moshe, and Avishai Margalit. *Idolatry*, trans. Naomi Goldblum. Cambridge: Harvard University Press, 1992.

Halevi, Yehudah. *The Kuzari: The Book of Refutation and Proof on Behalf of the Despised Religion,* trans. Barry S. Kogan and Lawrence M. Berman. New Haven: Yale University Press (forthcoming).

Hartman, David. *A Heart of Many Rooms: Celebrating the Many Voices Within Judaism.* Woodstock, Ver.: Jewish Lights, 1999.

———. *A Living Covenant: The Innovative Spirit in Traditional Judaism.* Woodstock, Ver.: Jewish Lights, 1992.

———. *Maimonides: Torah and Philosophic Quest.* Philadelphia: Jewish Publication Society, 1976.

Husik, Isaac. *A History of Medieval Jewish Philosophy.* New York: Meridian, and Philadelphia: Jewish Publication Society, 1958.

———. "The Philosophy of Maimonides," *Maimonides Octocentennial Series,* 4 New York: Maimonides Octocentennial Committee, 1935.

Maimonides, Moses. *Eight Chapters.* In *Ethical Writings of Maimonides.* Trans. Raymond L. Weiss with C. E. Butterworth. New York: New York University Press, 1975.

———. "Essay on the Resurrection of the Dead." In *Crisis and Leadership: Epistles of Maimonides.* Trans. Abraham Halkin, with discussions by David Hartman. Philadelphia: Jewish Publication Society, 1985.

———. *Guide of the Perplexed.* Trans. Shlomo Pines. Chicago: Chicago University Press, 1963.

———. "Kings and Wars," *The Code of Maimonides, Book Fourteen: The Book of Judges,* trans. Abraham M. Hershman. New Haven: Yale University Press, 1949.

———. "Laws Concerning Character Traits." In *Mishneh Torah.*

———. "Laws of Blessings." In *Mishneh Torah.*

———. "Laws of Divorce." In *Mishneh Torah.*

———. "Laws of Idolatry." In *Mishneh Torah.*

———. "Laws of Repentance." In *Mishneh Torah.*

———. "Laws of Sabbatical and Jubilee Years," *The Code of*

*Maimonides, Book Seven, The Book of Agriculture,* trans. Isaac Klein. New Haven: Yale University Press, 1979.

———. "Laws of Slaves." In *Mishneh Torah.*

———. "Laws of the Foundations of the Torah." In *Mishneh Torah.*

———. "Laws of the Study of the Torah." In *Mishneh Torah.*

———. *Mishneh Torah: The Book of Knowledge.* Edited according to the Bodleian (Oxford) Codex with introduction, biblical and talmudic references, notes, and English translation by Moses Hyamson. Jerusalem: Boys' Town, 1965.

*Mekhilta de-Rabbi Ishmael,* trans. Jacob Z. Lauterbach. Philadelphia: Jewish Publication Society, 1933.

*Midrash Rabbah: The Song of Songs,* trans. Maurice Simon. London: Soncino Press, 1961.

Muffs, Yohanan. *The Personhood of God: Essays in Biblical Religion* (forthcoming)

Pines, Shlomo "Shî'ite Terms and Conceptions in Judah Halevi's Kuzari," in *The Collected Works of Shlomo Pines,* ed. M. Idel and Z. Harvey, vol. 5. Jerusalem: Magnes Press, 1997.

Scholem, Gershom. *Major Trends in Jewish Mysticism.* New York: Schocken, 1965.

Soloveitchik, Joseph B. *On Repentance in the Thought and Oral Discourses of Rabbi Joseph B. Soloveitchik,* comp. and trans. Pinchas H. Peli. Jerusalem: Oroth, 1980.

Strauss, Leo. "The Law of Reason in the *Kuzari,*" in *Persecution and the Art of Writing.* Glencoe, Ill.: Free Press, 1952.

Weiser, Arthur. *The Old Testament Library: The Psalms.* Philadelphia: S.C.M. Press, 1962.

Wolfson, Harry. "Maimonides and Halevi," *JQR,* 2, no. 3 (January 1912).

Zimmerli, Walther. *The Old Testament and the World,* trans. J. J. Scullion. Atlanta, Ga.: John Knox Press, 1976.

# Index

Abraham: commitment to Halakhah, 79, 81–82; as educator, 60–61, 67–68, 70, 81; God, relationship with, 41–43, 65–68, 140–41; Halevi on, 41–42; and idolatry, 65–68; Maimonides on, 60–61, 65–68; and Moses, 69–70, 78

Adam, 59, 62, 117–18, 128

Aristotelianism: God, image of, 29, 43; Maimonides and, x–xi, 52–54, 59, 109–10, 142; and the Torah, 53

assimilation, 16–17, 20, 151–53, 158

Avineri, Shlomo, 17–18

Bible, the: on reward and punishment, 100–102; as source of legislation, 55–56, 74, 75; as text of Zionism, vii–viii, 3–10. *See also* Torah, the

Briggs, C. A., 106

Buber, Martin, 108

Christianity, 30–35, 85, 120

circumcision, 48, 78–79

community, covenantal: Jewish identity and, 130, 150–53, 155–57; mitzvah observance in, 48, 129–30; Torah study in, 160–65

Creation: Halevi on, 39–41, 128; Maimonides on, 118–22, 129–33; and revelation, 64, 128–33; and the uniqueness of the Jewish people, 39, 81, 128–29; universality of the narrative, 131–34, 137–38, 143. *See also* revelation; Sinai covenant

diaspora, 16–17, 20–24, 151–53, 158

*Eight Chapters* (Maimonides), 59, 146

election of Israel, 49, 71, 88, 137, 144, 156–57

exile, 2–3, 27, 32, 85–86, 94

Exodus, the Jews', 1–2, 38–39, 76–77, 96–98

God: Abraham's relationship with, 41–43, 65–68, 140–41; Halevi on, 37–40, 94; incorporeality of, 43, 84–85, 89–90, 92–93, 134–37; Israel, relationship with, 40, 49–51, 103–8, 130–31; in Jewish history, 7, 15, 94–98, 125; knowledge of, 68–69, 80–81, 84–85; Maimonides on, 37, 94; moral attributes of, 61–62; as teacher, 75–76, 105; worship of, 29, 39–40, 104–6. *See also* idolatry

God of the Philosophers, 29–31, 37, 43–44, 54, 85, 95

Greenberg, Moshe, 94, 106–7

*Guide of the Perplexed* (Maimonides): Aristotelianism in, 52–53; on circumcision, 78–79; on idolatry, 88; on mitzvoth, observance of, 54–55, 69–70; on moral attributes of God, 61–62

Halakhah: authority of, 47–49, 156–60; divine power described in, 98–99; as framework for Jewish life, 14–16, 125, 146, 164–65; Halevi on, 72, 83–84; on idolatry, 90–93, 98–100; Maimonides on, 79–84, 126, 132–33, 143; and *qorbanot*, 71–72; spirituality and, 79–80, 126. *See also* mitzvoth

Halevi, Yehuda: on the Creation, 39–42, 128; on election of Israel, 88; on exile, 27, 32, 85–86; on God, 37–40, 81, 94–95, 103; on Halakhah, 72, 83–84; on Land of Israel, 35–36, 49; on mitzvoth, observance of, 36, 45–48, 128; on philosophy, 34–35, 67, 86; on prophecy, 120–21; on *qorbanot*, 45–46, 71; on revelation, 40, 45–47, 88, 115–17, 128; on Sinai covenant, 117; on spirituality, 30–31, 40–41, 48; theology of, x–xii, 104, 108, 125. See also *Kuzari*

Hebrew language, xiii, 23, 27, 151–52

heresy, 89, 134

Heschel, Abraham Joshua, 136

Hirsch, Samson Raphael, 83

history: the Exodus, 38–39; God in, 7, 15, 38–39, 94–98, 125; Judaism in, 4–7, 13–15, 21, 32–35, 58; Maimonides on, 64, 125–26; messianism in, 33–34, 77–78; and rabbinic tradition, 96–97; and revelation, 62, 64, 70–71, 77

Holocaust, 22, 152, 153

*huqqim*, 45, 55–57, 72

Husik, Isaac, 52, 121

idolatry: Abraham's rejection of, 65–68; Halakhah on, 90–93, 98–100; Maimonides on, 64–65, 68–69, 88–93, 134–36; and moral behavior, 137–41; *qorbanot* in place of, 71–74; and worship, 64–65, 91–92, 136–37

Islam, 30–35, 85

Israel, Land of: Halevi and, 35–36, 49; Jews' biblical claim to, 128–29; return to, 2–3, 103–4

Israel, state of: diaspora relations with, 16–17, 23–25; Israel Independence Day, 153–54; and Jewish identity, 19–22, 127–28, 150–51, 157–58; moral vitality in, 144–47, 155; and peace process, viii, 9–11; polarization in, 11–12, 149–56, 165; rebirth of nationhood, 2–3, 24–25, 145–50; secularism in, viii–ix, 15–18, 126–28, 153–56, 158; Six-Day War, vii, 8–9, 123–25, 149, 155; and the Torah, 13–18; Yom Kippur War, 125. *See also* Zionism

Jews and Judaism: communalism, 20–21, 150–53, 155–57; in the diaspora, 16–17, 23–25; education, 60–61, 67–71; in history, 4–7, 13–15, 21, 32–35, 58; influence on

Christianity and Islam, 30–35; and knowledge of God, 68–69, 80–81, 84–85; and morality, 137–41; uniqueness of, 4–7, 39, 81, 128–29

Karaites, 50, 116–17
Kook, Abraham Israel, 145–46, 153–56
*Kuzari* (Halevi): on Christianity, 30–35; on the Creation, 39–42, 128; on exile, 27, 32, 85–86; on the Exodus, 38; on God, 28–30, 37–40, 94–95, 103; on Islam, 30–35; on Judaism in history, 32–35; on prophecy, 120–21

Leibowitz, Nehama, 84
Leibowitz, Yeshayahu, 140, 155
Levi, tribe of, 71, 80–81
Lieberman, Saul, 135

Maimonides, Moses: on Abraham, 60–61, 65–68; Aristotelianism and, x–xi, 52–54, 59, 109–10, 142; on the Creation, 118–22, 129–33; on election of Israel, 88, 156–57; on God, 37, 94–95, 126; on Halakhah, 79–84, 126, 132–33, 143; on history, 64, 94, 125–26; on idolatry, 64–65, 68–69, 88–93; on messianism, 82–84, 119–20; on mitzvoth, observance of, 54–58, 69–70, 127; on monotheism, 62; on nature, 62–64; and philosophy, 53–54; on prophecy, 120–21; *qedusha* as universal ideal, 81–82; on *qorbanot*, 72–75; on revelation, 58, 61–63, 129–30; on Sinai covenant, 59–62, 96, 131, 133–34; on spirituality, 109, 121; theology of, 104, 108. See also *Guide of the Perplexed; Mishneh Torah*
*Mekhilta*, 97–98, 130–31, 137–39
messianism: in history, 33–34, 77–78,

83; Maimonides on, 82–84, 119–20; and redemption, 145–46, 154; and return to the Land of Israel, 103–4
*Mishneh Torah* (Maimonides): on circumcision, 79; on idolatry, 88–92; on messianism, 82; on revelation, 62–63
*mishpatim,* 45, 55–56
mitzvoth: God's presence and, 107–8; Halevi on, 36, 45–48, 128; Maimonides on, 54–58, 69–70, 127; morality and, 59–60, 134, 137–38, 146–47; observance of, 36, 45, 69–70, 100, 126, 133; and Torah study, 12, 162
monotheism, 62, 64, 66–68
morality, 59–62, 134, 137–41, 146–47
Moses: and Abraham, 69–70, 78; as legislator, 61, 68–70, 120; as prophet, 69–70, 73, 120
Muffs, Yohanan, 106, 135

nature, 62–64, 100–101, 126

paganism. *See* idolatry
*pardes* studies, 63–64, 82, 113, 125
philosophy: God of the Philosophers, 29–31, 37, 43–44, 54, 85, 95; Halevi, 29–31, 34–35, 40, 43–45, 67, 86; Maimonides, 53–54
physics and metaphysics, 63–64, 82, 113, 125
Pines, Shlomo, 58, 86
prophecy: Halevi on, 115–17, 120–21; and idolatry, 69–70, 75; Maimonides on, 120; Moses and, 69–70, 73; and revelation, 95, 112

*qedusha,* 14, 81
*qiddush ha-shem,* 43
*qorbanot,* 45–46, 71–75

rabbinic Judaism, 95–97, 100–102, 108–14, 125

redemption: and Land of Israel, 36–37; messianism and, 9, 96, 145–46, 154

revelation: and the Creation, 128–33; Halevi on, 40, 45–49, 88, 115–17, 128; and history, 62, 64, 70–71, 77; Maimonides on, 58, 61–63, 129–30; in rabbinic tradition, 110–11; and Torah interpretation, 110–15, 121–22

reward and punishment, 100–103, 125

sacrifices. See qorbanot
Scholem, Gershom, 3–4, 54, 83, 88, 93, 126
secularism, viii–xi, 15–18, 126–28, 153–56, 158
Sinai covenant: Halevi on, 39, 117; Maimonides on, 59–62, 96, 131, 133–34
Six-Day War, vii, 8–9, 123–25, 149, 155
Soloveitchik, Joseph B., 152–56
spirituality: and Halakhah, 79–80, 126; Halevi on, 30–31, 40–41, 48; Maimonides on, 109, 121; and qorbanot, 46; Torah study and, 113
Strauss, Leo, 34–35

Talmud. See rabbinic Judaism
theology, 104, 108, 124–25

Torah, the: and Aristotelianism, 53; commitment to, 77, 79–81, 155–56; interpretation versus revelation, 110–15, 121–22, 160–63; in rabbinic Judaism, 108–14, 125; state of Israel and, 13–18; study of, 104–13, 160–62, 165; worship, as text of, 104–6

universalism: and the Creation narrative, 131–34, 137–38, 143; and mitzvoth, observance of, x, 58, 133–34, 143–44; qedusha as universal ideal, 81

Weiser, Arthur, 107–8
Wolfson, Harry, 53–54, 121
worship: of God, 39–43, 46, 50–51; idolatry, 64–65, 91–92, 136–37; and qorbanot, 71–74; Torah text as prayer, 104–6

Yad ha-Hazaqah (Maimonides), 52
Yom Kippur War, 125

Zimmerli, Walter, 94, 103
Zionism: anti-, 11; the Bible and, vii–viii, 3–10; religious, 8–11, 152–54; secular, 3, 9–10, 22–23; state of Israel and, 2–3, 24–25, 149–50